Woman
to
Woman

1,000 Conversation Starters for Talking about Anything

Kim Chamberlain

Skyhorse Publishing

Skyhorse Publishing books may be purchased in bulk at special discounts for sales promotion, corporate gifts, fund-raising, or educational purposes. Special editions can also be created to specifications. For details, contact the Special Sales Department, Skyhorse Publishing, 307 West 36th Street, 11th Floor, New York, NY 10018 or info@skyhorsepublishing.com.

Skyhorse® and Skyhorse Publishing® are registered trademarks of Skyhorse Publishing, Inc.®, a Delaware corporation.

Visit our website at www.skyhorsepublishing.com.

10 9 8 7 6 5 4 3 2 1

Library of Congress Cataloging-in-Publication Data is available on file.

ISBN: 978-1-62636-426-4

Printed in the United States of America

Woman
to
Woman

CONTENTS

INTRODUCTION

Why a conversation starters book specifically for women?

Within a short space of time women's conversation can cover many and varied topics and may include much laughter, intelligent observations on life, and a sharing of innermost thoughts.

While conversation in mixed company isn't always different, there are certainly times when the conversation's tone, the topics covered, and the depth of sharing is different in all-female company. Some topics are those that women would feel comfortable only discussing with other women in an empathetic, supportive, and non-threatening environment.

Although many conversation starters in the book can be used with both males and females, there are also many that are intended specifically for women, such as talking about your body, puberty, pregnancy, women and work, beauty, and other women.

This book is aimed primarily at situations where women are together having a conversation with other women, and builds on this situation by providing a wide range of questions and conversation starters that offer a great way to stimulate many types of discussion. Some topics may be ones that you regularly talk about, some may offer a new slant on a familiar topic, some may be ones you have wanted to talk about but have been uncomfortable about broaching, and others may be ones you hadn't thought about. All will most likely lead you into other conversation topics.

The book also touches on situations where you would use general conversation starters when you are out meeting people, say at a party or network event. A number of conversation starters, tips and techniques cover these issues.

A very easy book to dip into, *Woman to Woman* is suitable for adults and contains conversation starter topics that are thought-provoking, entertaining, controversial, factual, amusing, ridiculous, risqué, intellectual, and intimate. They provide the opportunity for fun, laughter, a way to learn new things, new ways of looking at issues, a chance to be listened to, a chance to work out what your thoughts are on a topic, a way to air issues you'd like to talk about, and an opportunity to discuss serious topics. They may allow you to open up new areas of discussion; perhaps discuss a subject you haven't been able to talk about before. You may be able to talk about issues you can't talk about with your partner or members of the opposite sex, along with the opportunity to develop your communication and thinking skills, and especially the chance to build a deeper level of connection and intimacy with others.

Speaking skills

Along with the hundreds of conversation starters, this book also offers insights into speaking skills, along with many tips and techniques incorporated throughout.

One of the ways to increase your speaking skills is first to become aware of speaking techniques. You may not, for example, have given any thought to issues concerning supportive feedback, interrupting, swearing, paraphrasing, how to avoid rambling, or different types of listening. Once you become aware of them and the factors involved, you then have a choice as to if and how you would like to develop your skills. The techniques will give you suggestions for ways to work on these skills.

USING THE BOOK

A benefit of this book is that you can use it for as long or short a period as you like, either in one-on-one situaitions or in a group. You can simply dip into it when you are with other females and want a bit of light-hearted conversation; you can use it for more in-depth conversations; you can use it for icebreakers; and you can create the right environment and use it as a way to build deeper connections with other women. You can even use the starters on your own to learn how to formulate responses, get to know your own thinking style, and work on your conversation skills.

1. How the book is organized

Speaking skills

The beginning of the book contains awareness-raising information on a range of speaking skills. This can help provide an understanding of some of the issues that are present in speaking and conversation. It also contains suggestions for developing skills in these areas.

Conversation starters

The starters are grouped into one hundred different topic sections, each containing ten questions and conversation starters.

The first topic section covers Easy Conversation Starters, simple starters that can be used in general situations. The others are in alphabetical order starting with "About You," weaving their way through many and wide-ranging topics, and ending with "Your Call!"

The starters fall into different types of categories, including ones that ask about you, "What was your favorite book as a child?"; ones that ask about your views or thoughts on issues, "Is social media helping or hindering *real* communication?"; ones that ask you to use your imagination, "In my wildest dreams this is what I would look like …"; and ones where people have to make guesses about you, "What types of pictures or posters did I have on my bedroom wall I was a teenager?"

At the end of the book is a page for you to make a note of any of your favorite starters or to compile some of your own.

Conversation tips and techniques

These are practical techniques you can use that will help improve conversation skills. They are included amongst the conversation starters.

There are three types of tips and techniques: Suggestions for asking good questions (Q); suggestions for answering questions (A); and general tips and techniques for conversation skills (G). They will have the letter (Q), (A) or (G) in front of each technique. Some give specific examples related to a particular conversation starter, though the techniques can be used in many circumstances.

2. A note on choosing conversation starters

Please note that some of the starters are not suited to beginning a "cold" conversation. Some starters cover, for example, personal matters, sensitive, controversial, or in-depth issues and are more suited to beginning a new topic during a conversation once things have warmed up, or with people you know well. Choosing these too early in a conversation may make others feel ill at ease, and may work against relationship-building. Choose starters that suit the people, the circumstances, and the flow of the conversation.

As a generalization, the type of starters that are more suited to opening a conversation, especially with someone you don't know, are ones of a general nature that don't delve too deeply into personal matters. This is explained later in "Understanding conversation levels," page 6.

In addition, be aware that some of the topics can produce an emotional response so you may need to check if others are happy to talk about them.

3. Suggestions for using the conversation starters

There are many ways to use the starters. Here are a few suggestions:

- You could have a themed conversation based on a topic area, for example "Beliefs," and work through all ten starters.
- You could have each person choose a different topic area and then choose a conversation starter from this area.
- You can use conversation starters more than once, for example with different people, or by asking another member of the group to start the conversation; this will probably make it go in a different direction.
- You could expand your way of communicating by speaking in the style of a different person, such as a person who has the opposite personality style to you (for example, someone who speaks fast, or uses a lot of pauses, or includes humorous anecdotes, or speaks

succinctly); someone from a different culture; someone from a different generation. This way you may find
other ways of speaking that suit you, as well as gaining
an understanding of how other people think and why
they speak as they do.

- You might like to practice improving your skills by using
role play where one person plays devil's advocate or
an angry person or an unwilling conversationalist, for
example, to help you practice the skill of dealing with
challenging conversations.

- You could specifically choose topics you are keen to
discuss and make time to have a conversation with
your daughter, sister, mother, grandmother, colleague,
or close friend, for example.

- You could arrange to have a conversation with people
from other backgrounds so that you can have a different conversation from your usual ones, or in order to
learn about the world they grew up (or are growing
up) in, and how their society and life experiences have
helped shaped their views and behavior. You could
choose people of different ages or from different cultures or different social settings.

- On a practical level, you could keep the book in your
bag or purse, in the glove compartment of your vehi-
cle or in your desk at work. Or you could keep a note
of a number of topics, for example, by writing a few
of them out or by taking a photo of them with your
phone, and keeping them with you to use when you
are with other women.

And so, here we go. Ready to get talking?

Happy conversations!

SPEAKING SKILLS

Many years ago I found myself in the office lunchroom with Todd, a man who worked in one of our other branches. Although I recognized him, I hadn't actually spoken to him before. He was the only person in the lunchroom, and as I sat down he looked up at me and uttered—in all seriousness—a conversation starter I will never forget: "So, what do you think of the debacle over the Icelandic fishing limit then?"

Some people are great conversationalists who make starting a conversation easy and effortless, and it's a pleasure talking to them. Others, like Todd, may like to learn a few simple ways to make starting a conversation easier for the other person.

Are great conversationalists born with an innate skill? Probably some people are more disposed to be good conversationalists than others, while there are also many people who have worked at polishing their skills. Don't worry if you think your skills aren't as good they could be; it's always possible to improve.

One of the main ways to improve is to practice—but make sure you are practicing the right things! Practicing the wrong thing will simply make you very skilled at whatever is not right.

Listed below, and included in the Conversation Starters, is a wide range of tips and techniques to help you work on your conversation skills.

1. Understanding conversation levels

Conversation generally operates on an agreed and unspoken set of rules. Often we don't realize that there *are* rules until we come across someone who operates outside of the accepted norm. One such person was Harry.

A former colleague of mine, Lucy, aged about 20, was a very chatty person who could talk about anything and everything. She was friends with Julie, also aged about 20, who was extremely quiet.

One day Lucy and Julie went for a drink, and as usual Lucy was happy to do the talking while Julie listened. After a while one of Lucy's friends, a young man named Harry, came and joined them. Harry hadn't met Julie before, and was also extremely quiet. Everything was going well, with Lucy chatting, and the other two listening, until Lucy decided to go to the bathroom. Realizing she was leaving her friends in a potentially uncomfortable situation, she leaned over to Harry and whispered "Don't sit there in silence, make some small talk," and off she went.

At this point Harry turned to Julie and asked, seriously, "So, are you a virgin then?"

Julie was appalled!

We know that what Harry did wouldn't be classed as "small talk." We also know from Julie's reaction that she deemed it "wrong." But why is it wrong? It's because Harry started off at the inappropriate level of conversation for the situation he was in.

The accepted norm is that conversation falls roughly into four levels, where people start off at Level One on meeting someone new and over a period of time—the length of which varies greatly from person to person—work through the levels. Harry, unfortunately, didn't start at Level One.

Level One: Small Talk

There are two main functions of small talk. Firstly, it's used as a "finding out" phase when we meet someone new. In small talk we chat about general issues, ones that anyone could easily talk about, such as the weather, in order to check out the other person. We use a somewhat bland conversation topic as a tool to see if there is any synergy with them, and then decide if we want to make a deeper connection.

When someone says "Isn't the weather great today?" or some such phrase, they are not asking about the weather, they are attempting to get a conversation under way and are using the ensuing exchange as a way to make a first impression of you. This impression is based on issues such as your general appearance, and how confident, trustworthy, friendly, reliable and intelligent you appear. The topic area "Easy Conversation Starters" in the Questions and Conversation Starters section on page 25 gives suggestions for small talk topics.

Secondly, it's a way to show acknowledgement of a friend or acquaintance without getting into deeper levels of conversation. For example, saying to a colleague on Monday morning as you are walking through the office "Hi, good weekend?" to which you expect a reply along the lines of "Yes, great, thanks," is using small talk as a politeness tool, a way to make a connection at a fairly surface level without the need for a longer conversation at that particular time.

People have different abilities when it comes to conversation skills, and different needs when it comes to conversing with others. This means that some people may stay at small talk level with others for a long time, possibly forever, while others may skip through the levels quite quickly.

Level Two: Factual Information

If we feel happy to progress further than small talk, the next level of conversation is where we share non-emotional factual information about ourselves. These are facts that will not cause either the speaker or the listener to feel uncomfortable. For example, we may talk about the work we do or the town where we live.

An example of a conversation at this level could be "I see you're new here." "Yes, we moved from New Orleans last month. My husband was transferred here with his job." Here, the second speaker has given away several pieces of non-emotional factual information regarding where she used to live, that she is married, and that her husband has been relocated with his work.

Level Three: Views and Opinions

At this level we start to open up, and may potentially go into "emotional" territory. Some people need to feel fairly comfortable with another person to converse at this level. They feel that if they share their views and opinions on an issue and the other person doesn't agree then there may be some element of rejection.

There are, of course, some people who don't care what others think of their views and opinions and will share them openly, regardless!

An example of Level Three could be a conversation regarding your thoughts about another person or a situation, your views on an item of news, or a sharing of your political or religious views.

Level Four: Personal Feelings

At this level we share our feelings; we share more of ourselves, and of who we really are. We may talk about our thoughts, dreams, fears, shortcomings. It's where we show a level of vulnerability, but it is where the deepest level of connection occurs.

An example could be a conversation between parents of school-age children: "I'm very worried about my son; he seems to be falling behind in his studies," or one between friends "I had some upsetting news from the doctor yesterday." If the other person is happy to converse at this level, they will not only talk through the stated concerns, but may also share some of their own issues.

People work their way through the levels at different rates, and sometimes in a different order. This may depend on a number of factors such as personality type, level of friendship, level of confidence, culture, or the circumstances they are in. Some people may like to stay at Small Talk level for the entire duration of their involvement with someone else, while others may be happy to get to Level Four within a couple of sentences. There is no right or wrong way, per se.

Poor Harry's problem was that he started a conversation in the depths of Level Four with someone he didn't know, who was extremely quiet and who was likely to take some time to open up to someone else. If Harry had been a confident, cheeky, fun-loving person and Julie had been similar, then she might have found his opening comment highly amusing and they might have launched into a great conversation. The issue was that Harry started off at the inappropriate level of conversation for the situation he was in.

The aim isn't to get to Level Four as soon as possible, nor is the aim to get to Level Four with everyone. The aim is to get to the level that both or all parties feel comfortable with at the time. Depending on the people and the circumstances, this may happen quickly, it may take some time, or it may not happen at all. A skilled conversationalist will aim to have a rewarding conversation at the level where all parties feel at ease.

The conversation starters in this book offer the opportunity to talk at any or all the four levels of conversation, so that you can move to whichever level(s) people feel comfortable with.

2.   Communication behaviors

There are four main ways we communicate with others. These are sometimes called Communication Behaviors and include aggressive, passive, assertive, and indirect or passive aggressive.

Let's use an analogy and imagine how four people, each displaying a different type of communication behavior, would enter someone else's house. The aggressive person would kick down the door and barge in, whether they were invited or not. The passive person would stay outside hiding behind the nearest bush, hoping someone would notice them and invite them in. The assertive person would simply go up to the front door, knock and wait to be invited in, while the indirect person would go round the back and climb in through the window.

How might this play out in a communication situation? Imagine that you have a manager at work who announces an open door policy. You go into the manager's office to have a word, but the manager doesn't look up. An aggressive person may respond by saying angrily, "You said you had an open door policy but you can't even be bothered to look up when people come in!" A passive person would wait, and wait, and wait. An indirect person would say nothing to the manager, but go back to their office and complain to others about the rudeness the manager had displayed, while an assertive person may say to the manager, "I see you're busy, when is a better time to have a talk with you?"

Taken to the extreme, these are ways that the four behavior types may operate:

Aggressive communicators express their needs and desires in a way that doesn't take into account the needs, desires or well-being of other people. They usually railroad others, talk over them, refuse to let them finish, criticize, and pay little attention to what they are saying.

Passive communicators are generally afraid of confrontation and don't feel they have the right to express their own views. They give in to other people's wishes and opinions even though they may not agree. They may also avoid saying what they want for fear of offending.

Indirect or passive aggressive communicators have difficulty expressing annoyance or disagreement in a healthy manner. They may appear kind and considerate on the surface but may harbor hurtful thoughts. They may make excuses, tell white lies, find underhanded means to get their own way, or agree with someone to their face and then be derisive or aggressive about them to others.

Assertive communicators express their thoughts, feelings, needs, and desires in an open and up-front way. They have the confidence to say what they want or mean, while considering and respecting the needs and desires of others.

Behaving assertively is generally the best way to communicate with others. When people adopt the other forms of communication behavior, it is usually due to a lack of self-esteem or because it's a learned behavior. The good news is that assertiveness is a learned skill. This means it's a behavior you can acquire, and can choose to use. When you choose assertive communication it will help you get to the point, communicate clearly as an equal, and express your views and feelings in a direct and appropriate way. Being assertive means you won't offend others and will have a healthy and respectful sense of control over situations.

One of the ways to develop assertive behavior is to "Act as if." Think of someone you know and respect who tends to communicate assertively. When you are in a situation where your natural inclination is to adopt one of the other three communication behaviors, ask yourself, "How would X behave in this situation?" Work out what he or she would do and "act as if" you were them. A benefit of doing this is that it may give you the sense that you are not tackling the situation on your own, but that X is there with you.

It will take some time "acting as if" until it becomes an ingrained behavior, however it is a very effective way to develop the skills. It's a case of fake it till you make it!

3.   It's not *just* what you say; it's how you say it

Conversation comprises two aspects, verbal communication and non-verbal communication.

The verbal aspect encompasses the words that are said while the non-verbal aspect covers the way people look, what people see them do (visual), along with how they sound (vocal), when they speak. Overall this means there are many factors going on that have the potential to lead to misunderstandings in conversation.

Recently my husband and I went to a café. On the counter was a sign saying FLAPJACKS with a plate of flapjacks next to it. There was also a sign saying BLUEBERRY MUFFINS, but with no muffins next to it.

"Do you have any blueberry muffins?" he asked.

"No, we haven't baked any yet," replied the woman.

"Then I think you might want this," he said, instantly picking up the BLUEBERRY MUFFINS sign and handing it to her.

After we sat down, I said that what he'd done had come across as a bit rude. My assumption was that he was feeling a bit irritated that there was a sign advertising something that wasn't available. He was surprised I saw it that way, as his intention was to save the woman the hassle of having other people ask the same question before the muffins were ready.

So often it's easy to make assumptions that aren't correct and not realize that we have misunderstood.

Meaning is contextual; we get the meaning from the context. Often, the context is wider than just the words that are said. It may be the physical or environmental context, or a context that is "invisible" such as someone's culture, experiences they have had in the past, or their thought processes. Unfortunately not everyone's context is the same. My context and my husband's were different in this instance. It wasn't significant this time, but in other situations it could be. You may be trying to be polite, and be seen as rude or aloof; you may be trying to be friendly and supportive, and be seen as interfering; you may be trying to give someone space, and be seen as uncaring. So many ways to be misunderstood!

While it's common for us to think about the words we say, and to sometimes choose them very carefully, it's less common to focus on our speaking style. Speaking style includes many visual and vocal issues such as eye contact, facial expressions, body language, intonation, use of pauses, how loud we speak, how much we speak, how fast we speak, how long we take to answer a question, whether we use social niceties, and subconscious use of regular phrases, for example apologetic or deferential expressions, along with interjections such as "um" and "er."

What can we do if we don't understand?

Being aware that there are many factors involved in communication and that we may have misunderstood will go a long way towards having good conversations and building strong connections with people. It's not uncommon, for example, for people to communicate in a roundabout way or not quite tell the truth because their main aim is to avoid upsetting the other person or causing damage to the relationship.

If something doesn't sound "right," bear in mind that the average person isn't aiming to offend and that our understanding of what they said, did, or how they looked, may not be what they meant.

A good place to start in these situations is to give people the benefit of the doubt. If it's not too serious we can let it go, making the assumption that they didn't mean any harm. Alternatively we could gently probe into what they meant. Ask questions for clarification, remembering to place the responsibility for understanding on yourself. This means saying something along the lines of "I'm not sure I understood; did you mean ...?" and not something like "You didn't express that very well."

What can we do if we aren't understood?

It usually seems obvious to us what we mean, and we may be confused as to why others don't see things as we do. A factor to bear in mind is that it may not have been the verbal or non-verbal factors that caused the misunderstanding, it may simply have been that the person wasn't listening properly and only heard part of what was said. However, if you find you are generally being misunderstood, one of the ways to deal with this is to reflect on the verbal and non-verbal aspects you use that could cause confusion, and then work out how to make amendments. For example, are you being too vague or too abrupt? Are you using so many pronouns ("he," "she," "him," "her," "they") without references to specific people that it's difficult to know who you're talking about? Perhaps you are speaking too rapidly or too softly, or you apologize too often. You may point at people too, rather than referring to them by name.

This may take some time to analyze and understand what to change. When you do change, however, people will respond to you differently. Asking a trusted friend to give you some honest feedback will be a help.

Another option is to consider amending your speaking style when you are with certain people; there may be things you do that act as distractors for them. For example, you may need to try enunciating more clearly, avoiding work jargon, changing your level of formality, eliminating swearing, having more eye contact, or speaking more slowly. Do this sensitively, though—you don't want to come across as patronizing.

Another alternative is, when appropriate, to present your message another way. Again, remember to place the responsibility for helping people understand on yourself. This means you may say "I don't think that came across as I intended; what I meant was . . ." rather than "You haven't understood."

4. Deeper meanings

Conversation also comprises another two aspects, information giving and interpersonal relationships.

Clayton Alderfer, American psychologist, developed the ERG theory (Existence, Relatedness, and Growth) to describe the main needs that humans have. "Existence" needs cover our basic material existence requirements; "Relatedness" needs cover our desire for interpersonal relationships; "Growth" needs cover our desire for personal development.

It's not uncommon to find that in many conversations the primary purpose is not the sharing of information but the social aspect, the building of relationships in order to feel connected to others. This means that while the words you say have a surface meaning (information), there may often be a deeper meaning at play, that of emotional connection.

People fall on a continuum when it comes to relatedness needs. For those at one end of the continuum, the need to feel connected to others is of paramount importance, while for those at the other end of the continuum there is little need to connect, and they prefer a more solitary existence. Most people will fall somewhere between the two. Where you are on the continuum will affect how you prefer to converse. If two people, one from each end of the continuum, were to have a conversation, one would see the giving and receiving of information as the only aspect to cover, while the other would see relationship building as the crux of the interaction.

There is no right or wrong to this; it's simply useful to understand the different ways that people communicate, and to take this into account when trying to work out the deeper meaning behind what they are saying.

When my daughter was little, I took her one day to visit our neighbor Kimberley, a very kindly woman. My daughter stood on a little plastic stool in her house, and a bit of it broke off.

"I'm really sorry," I apologized. "Some of the plastic has come off."

"No it hasn't, it's perfectly fine," Kimberley replied.

"But it's broken," I said, surprised that she couldn't see the damaged part.

"I don't see it," she said.

Eventually I realized that her primary concern wasn't the accuracy of the information I was providing, it was about the relationship. The deeper meaning she was conveying was that something as small as a broken part of a plastic stool wasn't worth worrying about, and that we should carry on our interaction, strengthening the relationship.

Understand that there will be times when what people are saying relates more to the deeper meaning of interpersonal relationship than it does to the surface meaning of information sharing.

5. How to avoid rambling

The Canadian humorist Stephen Leacock wrote about a man who "flung himself upon his horse and rode madly off in all directions." Do you speak like this? Do you tend to fling yourself into a topic of conversation without much thought, then ramble and go off on tangents while you are talking? Or do you find that you start on a topic without an idea of where your thoughts are heading and are not sure of the point you are trying to make?

If so, the following 3-step technique will help you avoid this and speak with impact. While a simple technique, it may take a few attempts to become skilled at it:

1) Pause
2) Work out your end point
3) Go in a straight line

To avoid going off on a tangent when you are asked a question, first pause for a few seconds before you start speaking. This pause provides two main benefits. Firstly it gives you a chance to work out the rough outline of what you are going to say. Secondly it gives the impression that you are going to give a considered response. People will then give more weight to what you say.

During the pause, work out the end point of what you are going to say, that is, the overall message you want to give. Perhaps you may also be able to quickly formulate an overview of the ideas you want to present. If you do this, you will avoid starting to talk without a direction to go in. You will be able to speak "in a straight line" which will significantly reduce rambling. Make sure you have a point you are making; it need only be one point, and the stronger the better.

It's also useful to know when to stop. There is no point in speaking for the purpose of making a noise! People favor to-the-point responses and generally prefer not to listen to long, waffling monologues. Make your point, then stop talking and let others contribute.

6. Using a framework to structure your speaking

If there is a topic that requires some thought which you would like to address it in a fairly structured way, one way to organize your thoughts is to use a framework.

For example, a Before & After framework.

Let's say the conversation starter is *"What kinds of problems are you skilled at helping others with?"* One of the ways to answer this could be to use a Before & After framework. Talk about how things were before, what happened, and then how things have been since then. For instance, your response may be along the lines of "Before I split up with my partner I didn't have much understanding of how to live on a very limited budget. Now that I'm separated I've had to learn many strategies for bringing up children on a shoestring, and I've built up a lot of information I can share with women in a similar situation."

Or a Past Present Future framework.

If the conversation starter were *"Within your society, what level of acceptance is there for gay females?"* you could start by explaining how the situation used to be in the past, how things have changed to the current situation, and what you expect will happen in the future.

Or a Belief Reason Suggestion framework.

This is where you express your views, and then give the reason to support them, followed by advice or suggestions.

For example, with the conversation starter *"Does marriage counseling work?"* you might say you believe that it does help, the reason being that simply taking time out to discuss issues can be of benefit in itself, over and above what the counselor may say, and suggest that anyone interested could book an initial session to see if it may work for them.

There are many types of frameworks you can use, including:

Before & After
Past Present Future
Belief Reason Suggestion
Goals Obstacles Solutions
Problem, Solution
Advantages & Disadvantages
Cause and Effect
Anecdote
Financial Cost and Social Cost
Local National International
The Ideal and the Reality or Likelihood
Civil Law, Moral Law
Cost and Benefit
Personal Experience
Start with an opinion then justify or explain it
Narrow the topic down
Split the topic into components
Low Medium High
How What Where When Who Why
Us Them

1,000 QUESTIONS AND CONVERSATION STARTERS

This section contains one hundred different topic sections, each containing ten conversation starters. It begins with "Easy Conversation Starters," which are simple starters that can be used in general situations, followed by the remaining ninety-nine sections in alphabetical order.

Incorporated throughout the starters are tips and techniques for improved conversation skills. Those covering tips for questions have a (Q) before them; those covering tips for answers have an (A) before them; and those covering general conversation tips have a (G) before them.

At the end is a section where you can list your favorite starters and include any of your own.

Easy conversation starters

About you

Advice

Age

Animals

Anything and everything

Beauty

Beliefs

Books

Business

Business Partnerships

Career

Childhood

Children

Comfort Zone

Communication

Confidence
Conflict
Coping strategies
Creativity
Dating
Do you like ... ?
Dreams and hopes
Education
Either/Or
Emotions
Entertainment
Family and family life
Fashion, clothes and makeup
Fears
Flirting
Food and drink
Friendships
Fun
Health
Hobbies and interests
House and home
In my wildest dreams!
International Issues
Irritations
Is it appropriate ... ?
It's the Little Things
Leaving this World
Let's guess!
Love
Marriage
Meeting with Friends
Men
Mixed bag

Money
Movies
Music
Names and numbers
Other women
Paranormal
Personality
Physical appearance
Pleasure
Politics
Possessions
Pregnancy
Previous relationships
Problems
Quotes about Women
Quotes by Women
Reactions
Relationships
Romance
School
Secrets
Sex
Shopping
Situations
Spiritual
Star Signs
Stay at Home Mom
Stories
Strangers
Stress
Support
Technology
Teenage years

Temptation

The Common Good

The future

Time

Treating yourself

Truth and Lies

Understanding Behavior

Vacations and travel

Weird and wonderful

What would you do if ... ?

Wisdom

Women Achievers

Women and work

Women Who ...

Work-life balance

Worrying

Your call!

Plus ... Your Favorites & Your Starters

Easy Conversation Starters

You may need to amend these starters to fit the situation.

- The weather's great / terrible / unusual at the moment, isn't it?
- Are you from this area?
- Have you got family around here?
- Do you work?
- Are you planning a vacation this year?

(Q) Start a conversation with easy questions

This technique is especially good to use with people you don't know well. Easy questions are the kind of general questions that anyone can answer. They are ones of a general nature that don't require any specific knowledge and are "non-threatening" topics that don't delve into personal details or cover contentious issues. They fall into the "Level One, Small Talk" level of conversation (page 7).

Example

Topic: Easy conversation starters

Starter: *The weather's very unusual for this time of year, isn't it?*

- I like your outfit / necklace / scarf . . . where did you get it?
- How was your Christmas / Thanksgiving / Easter break / weekend?
- Did you see the Super Bowl / the news on TV today / the final episode of . . . ?
- Have you been here / to this type of meeting / to Poppy's house . . . before?
- How do you know Rachel / Carol / name of host or mutual friend . . . ?

(Q) Talk about the environment

When beginning a conversation, particularly with someone you don't have much conversation history to call on, talking about an aspect of the environment you're in is a good starting point. You could talk about the type of event you're at, the building you're in, the scenery, the speaker, the people, the food, the music . . .

Example

Topic: Easy Conversation Starters

Starter: *Have you been to one of Jackie's parties before?*

About you

- Do you have any brothers and sisters?
- Do you remember people's birthdays?
- How would you finish this sentence: People say I'm good at . . .
- Which three adjectives would best describe you?
- Do you tend to avoid letting people know that you're good at something and hide your light under a bushel, or does modesty play no part and you sing about it from the hilltops?

(Q) Many people like to talk about themselves!

People generally find it easy to talk about themselves, so a simple fact-finding question is a good topic to start with. We all like to feel that someone is interested in us. Always follow up with more questions about them, and avoid turning the conversation back to yourself instantly.

Example

Topic: About You

Starter: *Do you have brothers and sisters?*

- Have you ever done something silly that you regretted?
- What couldn't you live without?
- Do you like your name?
- Have you had a traditional or a non-traditional life so far?
- Have you ever faced an obstacle in your life and overcome it?

(Q) Open vs. closed questions (1)

A closed question can lend itself to a one-word or short answer. Closed questions are okay to use some of the time, though don't use them too much.

Example

Topic: About You

Starter: *Do you like your name?*
The other person could answer, for example, *"Yes," "No,"* or *"Sort of."*

If you know that the person is prone to regularly giving short answers, try amending the question to be more open, for example *"What do you think about your name?* Or be ready to follow up a short answer with an open question, such as *"Were you named after someone?"*

Advice

What advice would you give in these scenarios?

- Your mom is sixty-five and wants to do a university degree, purely for interest's sake. It will mean that she has to spend most of her savings to be able to fund it. She's eager, but you're not so sure, as your family has a history of living to a great age.
- Your friend is in her fifties, and her face is starting to show the signs of aging. She isn't happy about getting older and is wondering if she should get a facelift.
- Your sixteen year old son wants to learn to ride a motorcycle. You have the finances to pay for lessons for him, but are worried about the safety issues involved.

(Q) Let people answer. It's okay to have silence for a while

Once you've asked a question, give the other person time to think. Not everyone can give an answer straight away, and you don't need to fill in the silence. People are more likely give a well-thought out answer if they know you are going to give them thinking time and not rush them to respond.

- Your friend's hobby is ballroom dancing, which she loves. However it takes up a large amount of her time and there is a lot of traveling involved. She finds it a struggle to also cope with a full-time, demanding job, and doesn't feel she can handle both for much longer.
- Your friend has always said that she wouldn't marry, but would happily live with someone. The partner she

has been living with for three years has asked her to marry him. She loves him and wants to stay with him but doesn't see the point of getting married. He is feeling hurt about this.

- Your mom has been widowed for five years and is still young at heart. Your sister would like her to consider dating but your mom is a bit shy and unsure if she could do it.
- Your parents have had a huge win on the Lottery and are wondering what to do with the money.

(G) Giving support—agreeing

You can give support to others by showing agreement with their views or thoughts. You can either do this directly "I completely agree with that" or indirectly "I think Heather's views make a lot of sense."

- Your colleague has been offered a promotion which will mean moving five hundred miles away. She wants the job, but has never lived outside of her home town where all of her family live. She's worried she will miss them, and vice versa. She is single with no children.
- Your friend has a small child, and she and her partner would like to have another. However her sister, to whom she is very close, is unable to have children and would find it distressing if she were to have another child.
- Your husband is unhappy in his job despite being highly regarded by colleagues and management. He would dearly love to do a completely different type of work. This would require two years' re-training, and the job itself would be significantly lower paid.

Age

- What would appeal to you most about being a child again?
- When did you feel you had changed from an adolescent into a woman?
- Do you feel mature?
- How would you finish this off: If I were ten years younger . . .
- What are your thoughts about menopause?

(A) Invitation to speak.

Conversation consists of turn-taking. One of the ways to indicate it's someone else's turn when you've finished speaking is to invite them to speak. For example by finishing with *"Don't you think so?" "What would you have done?"* or asking them the question they asked *you "And what about you, how would you respond to 'If I were ten years younger'. . . ?"*

- What physical signs of aging have you noticed?
- Do you try to hide your age in any way?
- At what age were you happiest?
- What are the advantages of getting older?
- What are the disadvantages of getting older?

(Q) Be careful about asking several questions at once

Sometimes it's okay to ask a couple of related questions at the same time. For example, you might ask a closed question that requires a short answer, along with an open one that will allow the other person to expand on what they've said. For example: *Do you procrastinate? And if so, when?*

However, if you ask several open questions, or several questions that require fairly different answers, people won't know which one to answer. Just ask the one question and leave space for them to speak. You can ask the other questions as the conversation continues.

Example

Topic: Age

Starter: *Do you try to hide your age in any way?*

NOT: *Do you try to hide your age in any way? What are your thoughts on plastic surgery when you're older? And what about Betty, do you think she's had a facelift?*

Animals

- Do you like animals?
- What pets have you had during your life?
- Other than pets, have animals been a part of your life?
- Are you familiar with any incidents of cruelty towards animals?
- Are there any creatures that you are afraid of?

(G) Going off on a tangent (1)

If someone starts to go off on a tangent when you haven't finished the topic, one option is to let them know you'll come back to what they are saying in a minute.

- Have you been, or would you like to go, on a wildlife safari?
- Do some people have animals as substitutes for children?
- Is it okay to house animals in a zoo?

- What are your views on vegetarianism?
- What are your views on hunting?

Anything and everything

- If I were ruler of the country for a week I would . . .
- I laughed so much when someone told me . . .
- On a scale of zero to ten, what score would you give yourself for being a risk taker?
- I love the smell of . . .

(Q) Ask the question without rambling

Ask the question and then stop and let the other person answer. You don't need to keep adding to the question.

Example

Topic: Anything and Everything

Starter: *On a scale of zero to ten what score would you give yourself for being a risk taker?*

NOT: *On a scale of zero to ten what score would you give yourself for being a risk taker? Are you maybe a ten . . . or would you put yourself a bit lower at eight? Or perhaps . . .*

- Are you forgetful?
- If you had to marry a famous person, who would you choose?
- If it were possible to eat any type and amount of food as you liked, without it being bad for you in any way, what would your diet consist of?
- Which of these options sounds the most appealing? Spending a year:

o   Working in the Antarctic as a researcher
o   Fostering three teenage children
o   Writing a biography of a living public figure
o   Training to be—and working as—a comedienne
o   Studying yoga and meditation

(G) Bonding: Use the other person's name (1)

When first meeting someone it's good to use the other person's name. Use it when you first hear it, *"Hi Anne, good to meet you"* and use it again early in the conversation. This will help you remember their name and show you are interested in them. It will begin the bonding process.

Example

Topic: Anything and Everything

Starter: *If you had to marry a famous person, who would you choose?*

TRY: *What about you, Anne, if you had to marry a famous person who would you choose?*

- Do you look at clouds and work out what they look like?
- In some cultures, it is the grandparents—not the parents—who raise the children. When the parents become grandparents, they take on the role of bringing up the next generation. Does this sound like a good idea?

(G) Don't drag out a conversation

Sometimes a conversation comes to a natural end. Don't feel you have to drag it out any longer just for the sake of it. You can finish on a positive note and move on, or change the topic, or suggest you go and do something like have a cup of coffee

Beauty

- What's your beauty regimen?
- Do you spend a lot on beauty products?
- If you could have any plastic surgery you wanted for free, what, if anything, would you have done?
- When have you felt at your most beautiful?
- Who would you describe as being physically beautiful?

(G) Bonding: Use the other person's name (2)

Using the other person's name from time to time will help with bonding, but if you overdo it, it makes people feel uneasy, and will probably sound like you are trying to sell them something!

For example if you are talking about beauty regimens, avoid saying something like *"I think, Joy, that your beauty regimen is very impressive, and Joy, have you ever tried making your own coconut face mask? Joy, I tried it once, and it was . . ."*

- Tell us about someone who has a beautiful personality.
- Do you surround yourself with beautiful things?
- Describe the most beautiful place you've been to.
- Is there too much emphasis on beauty?
- Why does beauty sell?

(G) Bonding: Use the other person's name (3)

Referring to another person in a positive way is a good way to show respect for them. *"I really like the beautiful artifacts that Gillian has in her house. She's very good at surrounding herself with items she loves . . ."*

Beliefs

- When we are children sometimes we believe or think things that we later realize aren't correct. Did you have any of these childhood beliefs?
- When you were a child, did you believe in Santa and the Tooth Fairy? Anything else?
- Do you have religious beliefs?
- Can you think of a time when you didn't believe someone but it later turned out to be true?
- Were you brought up in a family with particular religious beliefs?

(Q) Keeping the questions general

There are times when you have the choice of narrowing a question down, or making it more general. Sometimes it's useful to keep the questions general as there may be aspects you haven't considered that the other person wants to talk about.

Example

Topic: Beliefs

Starter: *Do you have religious beliefs?* is a more general question than *Are you a Christian?*

- What thoughts have you had about religion as you have gone through life?
- Do you pray, or do something similar?
- Do you believe in reincarnation?
- It's said that we question all of our beliefs, except for the ones we *really* believe. Agree?
- What's the difference between Christianity and Islam?

(Q) Avoid starting a conversation with a criticism

It's generally a good idea to start a conversation with a positive or neutral approach. Starting with a criticism, especially if it's an issue the other person holds dear, can cause ill feeling.

Example

Topic: Beliefs

Starter: *Do you believe in reincarnation?*

NOT: *Don't you think that people who believe in reincarnation are dumb?*

Books

- How big a part do books play in your life?
- What was your favorite book as a child?
- What is your favorite book of all time?
- Do you remember your teacher reading a book out loud to the class at school?

(G) Shy people—speak first!

If you have a tendency to be shy and usually wait until someone else starts speaking, begin training yourself to speak first. Set yourself small goals initially, maybe to start first just once a week. Learn a couple of simple conversation starters and use those. Increase your goals as you achieve your initial ones.

- Have you ever read a book and then seen the movie of it? How did they compare?
- Do you have a fictional counterpart? Which character in a book or a movie is most like you?

- If you were given a contract to write any kind of book at all, what book would you write?
- Tell us about a book that you couldn't put down.

(G) Going off on a tangent (2)

If someone goes off on a tangent, there are times when this is okay as it can lead to an interesting line of discussion.

- Name all the places where you keep books and reading material.
- It's said that a third of high school graduates never read another book for the rest of their lives. Why? And are they missing out?

Business

- If you wanted to set up in business and needed $100,000 to get it off the ground, how would you go about finding a funding source?
- You want to open up a beauty parlor and spa on the main street of the town where you live. Some lovely premises have become available but are neighbored by a fast food outlet often frequented by noisy teenagers, and a tattoo parlor often frequented by bikers. Would you take them?
- Would you be willing to work seven days a week in the early days of setting up a business?
- It is said that, in general, women set up smaller businesses than men. Why is this?
- Is it possible to be feminine and successful in a male dominated business?

(G) Including others

If someone in the group is very quiet and tends not to proffer information, include them by asking questions or asking their opinion from time to time. They may have something very interesting to contribute.

- How big a part is social media playing in business growth at the moment?
- What are the characteristics a woman may need to become CEO of a large organization?
- Why do businesses need to have a unique selling point?
- Is it okay for large businesses to headhunt from smaller businesses?
- Think of a multinational business. What's its competitive advantage?

Business Partnerships

The following people would like to go into business together using their skills, knowledge and experience to do something different to what they are doing at present. What suggestions could you give as to options that might be worth considering?

- Mother and daughter. The mother works as a kindergarten teacher, enjoys helping children learn, loves planning, variety in the workplace and crafts. The daughter works in a garden center, enjoys physical and practical work, likes being in nature and in peaceful environments.
- Husband and wife. The husband is a real estate agent who thrives on working towards business success. He is good at sales and dealing with finances and would like a change from dealing with face-to-face clients. He

wants to be based in an office full time. The wife is an accountant. She enjoys dealing with people, problem solving, logic, order and methods. She wants to move away from working with finance and figures and is interested in a more "caring" work situation.

G) When to say nothing

There is a quote "A wise man once said . . . absolutely nothing because sometimes it's wisest to keep your mouth shut".

Yes, there are times when the best form of communication is to say nothing. You don't always have to say something, and silence may be by far the most suitable option. It may take a lot of self-control to avoid saying those unkind words that are on the verge of coming out, but bite your tongue and say nothing. You will know when those times are. It's good to learn the discipline of saying nothing when appropriate, and you will be forever grateful for having kept quiet.

- Brother and sister, both young and single. The brother works in a camping store. He is keen on most outdoor sports, particularly in skiing, surfing, kayaking and hiking. He hates paperwork and phone work and wants to be outdoors all the time with groups of people. He doesn't care what the working hours are. The sister works as a swimming instructor. She also loves racquet sports, especially tennis, badminton and squash. She likes being with people, teaching and training them and would be keen on having a café as part of whatever business they set up.
- Two work colleagues, female. Colleague One is a manager in a bank who doesn't find the day-to-day tasks stimulating. She is a voluntary mentor for newer bank staff, and finds this the most enjoyable part of the job.

She wants to work in the field of personal development, and have more variety and flexibility in her work. Colleague Two is also a bank manager in a different branch. She likes the rigid structure of the job, enjoying most of the tasks, but wants to be her own boss rather than an employee. She has great organizational skills and likes new challenges. She has a strong interest in acting and dancing but has never considered bringing this into her work.

(G) Repetition

The best type of situation for people to learn in is one where they *want* to learn, and where there is repetition of the message. This means that if you want to specifically get your message across, you may need to repeat it.

Of course this won't always be the case. If you say something dramatic such as *"I've just inherited a lot of money and I want to give you a million dollars,"* it's highly likely you won't need to repeat that. However, in normal conversation where a lot of information of similar "weight" is being exchanged, your message may get lost if you don't repeat it.

- Two university students, male and female. The male student is studying German and Italian and has a natural aptitude for languages, both spoken and written. He likes to travel, is interested in technology and would like a business that allows him to use technology in an innovative way. The female student is studying English and runs a university group that produces a regular magazine. She is happy to be office-based, researching, collecting and collating information. She is particularly interested in overseas aid agencies.

- A family: mother, father and son. The mother is a housewife, very involved in all local groups, schools and the church in their small home town. She loves baking, gardening and all home crafts. The father works in a barbershop, a very popular figure who is interested in people. He is one of the leading lights in Rotary, the local choir, and the church, and people often come to talk to him when they have problems. The son runs a teenage youth group at church, spends a lot of time playing sports with friends, and ultimately wants to become a missionary teacher.

- Two sisters. Sister One works in a health food store. She spends most of her free time in the gym or running. She loves to keep fit and eat well. She doesn't like to relax and thinks that life is about being active. Sister Two is a clerical assistant who likes clothes, jewelry, shoes, make-up, and hair. She thinks it's important to look good on the outside as it helps people feel good on the inside. She has no formal qualifications but spends a lot of time reading glossy magazines and working out what's current.

(G) Looking relaxed

People tend to pick up on others' emotions. Generally people want to feel at ease, which means that if you present as being ill-at-ease and are playing with your hair, wiggling your foot or changing sitting position regularly, then they will feel ill at ease too.

Unless there is a major reason for feeling unsettled, aim to look as relaxed as you can. Simply being aware that you are not relaxed is the first step towards being able to make a few changes. Take a few low, slow breaths; do a quick check of how relaxed you may or may not look; mentally take the tension out of any tensed parts of your body, and try to "think" yourself into a more relaxed frame of mind.

- Two friends, male. Friend One plays in a band in the eve-
nings and at the weekend. He loves music and has a huge
collection of records, CDs and music memorabilia. He
would hate a day job, preferring to sleep in the morning, and hang out late at night with other musicians after
the band has performed. His other passion is coffee and
he has several coffee machines at home. Friend Two is a
college music tutor who spends his spare time writing
music and going to music gigs in cafes. He would like a
structured business where the focus is on making money.

- Two neighbors, female. Neighbor One is a stay at home
mom who loves recycling, upcycling, and making do.
She dislikes the concept of waste and feels that people
could reduce their consumerism in order to make
the world a better place. She can turn her hand to
most practical tasks, and would like a part-time business to fit in with child care. Neighbor Two is a part
time graphic designer, working mainly with charitable
organizations. She sees the beauty in most things and
would like the world to be a more colorful place. She
wants a business that makes her feel she is contribut-
ing to the general good of the community, particularly
to making the environment more beautiful.

- Father and son. The father is an IT consultant who
enjoys project management, electronics, gadgets and
all things IT. He is also skilled at practical work and
does a lot of DIY, electronic and building projects at
home. He is not interested in sales work. The son is an
engineering student who is interested in electronics,
gadgets, computer gaming, videos, films, podcasts, and
anything related to technology. Both are good at communicating with others and are happy to work long
and unsocial hours.

Career

- Give a brief overview of your career. Has it panned out how you hoped it would?
- What future career plans do you have?
- Other than qualifications, what else do you need to be, do or have, in order to succeed in your chosen field(s)?
- Which have been your best and worst jobs?
- Who has been your best boss?

(G) Listening skills: Minimal Encouragers

Minimal encouragers are very simple actions that show the other person you are listening; that you are interested in what they are saying; and that you are "encouraging" them to continue.

Minimal encouragers include such things as nodding, saying phrases like *"yes" "sure" "uh-huh" "okay"*, showing interest or surprise *"wow!"*, and slightly leaning forward when something interests you.

People don't tend to notice minimal encouragers when they happen, but you notice when they are missing. In situations where you have been speaking for a while and the other person hasn't offered any minimal encouragers, you may start wondering if there is an issue *"Am I boring her?" "Have I said something incorrect?" "Is she listening?"*

If minimal encouragers aren't yet part of your conversation tool kit, start to bring them in.

- How did you choose your first job?
- Have you earned the income you feel you deserve?
- Which suits you better: business, self-employment or employment?
- Tell us about some interesting or unusual colleagues you've had.
- Do you plan to retire? If so, when?

(Q) Rephrase

If the starter is phrased in a different way to how you would say it, or in a way that isn't appropriate for the other person, it's okay to rephrase it.

Example

Topic: Career

Starter: *Do you plan to retire? If so, when?*
If the person has already retired, you might say, *"When did you retire? And had you planned this?"*

Childhood

- When you were a child, who was your best friend?
- Was your childhood happy?
- Which was your most memorable birthday?
- What happened when you argued with your friends?
- Which were your favorite TV or radio programs?

(Q) Answering a closed question in an open way

Some of the questions in the book are deliberately phrased as closed questions, designed to let you practice closed *or* open responses.

A closed question generally produces a short response, while an open question produces a longer response. Not everyone is skilled at asking open questions, and you may find yourself in a conversation where the other person asks many closed questions. In these cases it's useful to be able to take a closed question and give a full response.

Example

Topic: Childhood

Starter: *Was your childhood happy?*

This is technically a closed question that could produce a one word response, *"Yes," "No,"* or *"Sometimes,"* for example. What would work better in this instance is to give a fuller response to get—or keep—the conversation going. For example, *"I have some lovely memories of my childhood. Like the times we would go to the beach over the summer and spend most of the time in the water..."*

- What did you want to be when you grew up?
- What was your bedroom like when you were a child?
- Which was your favorite toy?
- When you were a child, what was your most favorite thing in the world to do?
- Did you have any childhood illnesses?

(Q) Start your answer with a story or anecdote

Using a short story or anecdote is an easy way to begin talking about a topic as it's something that doesn't require much thinking. People love to hear stories, especially amusing, heart-warming, intriguing or shocking ones, and ones they can relate to.

Example

Topic: Childhood

Starter: *Which was your favorite toy?*

Instead of replying *"My favorite toy was a jigsaw puzzle"* you could start with a story: *"One day when I was six years old, my dad came home with something hidden inside his jacket..."*

Children

NOTE: Please be considerate when using this topic; it may be a sensitive area for some women. Check if it's okay to talk about these issues.

- When you were growing up, did you want to have children?
- How has having children changed your life?
- What do you love most about your children?
- What do your children do that drives you mad or disappoints you?
- Given a complete choice, how many children would you have? Why this number?

(Q) If you think it may be a sensitive topic for someone

Be aware that certain topics may be sensitive areas for some people, depending on their situation; for example topics about children, pregnancy, marriage and money. Check if they are happy to talk about this topic. If not, go on to something else.

- How would you finish this off: Children these days ...
- What needs to be done to combat childhood obesity?
- Are children of celebrities and royalty spoiled?
- Do parents pander too much to their children?
- What effect does TV advertising have on children?

(G) Giving support—empathy

You can give emotional support by showing empathy with others, for example: *"Oh my goodness, I know exactly how you feel, the same thing happened to me and I can understand what you're going through."*

Sympathy and empathy are not the same. Being sympathetic means offering consolation when someone is dealing with an issue you haven't necessarily experienced. Being empathetic is when you appreciate the challenges someone has had because you have experienced them yourself.

Comfort Zone

You've been asked to step outside of your comfort zone. Which of these would be more challenging for you, and what would you like to have in place to help you to do it?

- Picking up a large spider or giving a presentation to a thousand people?
- Spending twenty-four hours in solitary confinement or hang gliding?
- Going to a party on your own or doing a five minute slot as a warm-up act for a comedian?
- Sleeping in a haunted castle or going down a cat walk modeling underwear?
- Sitting in a bath full of snakes or going on the world's largest roller coaster?

(G) Chunking

People like things when they are packaged in chunks. If you have a lot to say, you don't need to burble it out in one long monologue.

Split it into chunks. Divide what you want to say into manageable and logical segments, such as stages of an issue or problem, of what happened in the past, what's happening now, and what is likely to happen in the future. People will understand it more and will be less likely to lose interest if you break it up.

- Spending an hour in an isolation tank (a lightless, soundproof tank where you float in salt water) or watching an operation?
- Rappelling one hundred feet down the outside of a building or being trapped in the ghost train tunnel for three hours?

- Having your hair shaved off for charity or having a TV crew film every room in your house without giving you a chance to tidy up?
- Having someone post an embarrassing photo of you on Facebook or being an assistant to a knife-throwing magician?
- Spending a week wearing baggy, scruffy, unflattering clothes without makeup or jewelry, or eating a meal of sheep's eyeballs, boiled grasshoppers, and fried caterpillars?

Communication

- Do you use snail mail?
- If you are on Facebook, how do you use it?
- If you want to ask a friend a non-urgent question, would you call them, go to see them, email them, text them, or contact them in another way?
- Imagine you had to speak at an event in front of an audience of five hundred people for thirty minutes. How would you feel?

(Q) Open vs. closed questions (2)

Open questions tend to lead to longer answers, and are good to keep the conversation flowing. You can change a closed question to an open one if you prefer.

Example

Topic: Communication

Starter: Compare *"Do you use snail mail?"* which can lead to a *"Yes"* or *"No"* answer, with *"When did you last write a letter to someone and mail it to them?"* which is likely to lead to a longer answer.

- Do you think you can generally tell when people are telling the truth?
- If a friend asked what you thought of her new outfit, and you thought it didn't suit her at all, would you tell her?
- If you are having coffee with someone and a friend calls you on your cell phone, is it okay to answer the phone and have a conversation with them?

(G) Actively listen

There is a difference between hearing and listening. Hearing is passive, while listening is active. This means that you need to be actively paying attention to what others are saying.

If you have had the experience of being in a conversation and unable to answer a question as you have let your mind wander, you have probably heard the sound of conversation in the background, though were not actively listening.

A good way to stop your mind wandering is to ask questions from time to time, or use minimal encouragers (page 43).

- Have you ever been too shy to say what you really wanted to say?
- Is social media helping or hindering real communication?
- Large organizations regularly cite "communication" as one of the problems that impedes efficiency. Why is this?

Confidence

- Which aspect of your life are you the most confident about?
- Do you find confidence an attractive trait in a potential partner?

- One of the ways to increase confidence is to "borrow" it from someone who is confident, by acting as if you were them. Have you ever done this?
- Think about all the members of your family. Who is the most confident and who is the least?
- Some women link their level of confidence to how they feel about their body and some women don't. Do you?

(G) Don't aim to impress

When having a conversation, the aim isn't to impress others, be able to ask "clever" questions, or show how wonderful you are! To have a great conversation one of the most important aspects is to simply be friendly.

If you are friendly people will usually respond accordingly and you will be able to start forming a bond. Good bonds lead to good conversations, and vice versa.

- Why do some teenage girls lose the confidence they had when they were children?
- What's the difference between a pleasant level of confidence and over-confidence?
- What is the main cause of lack of confidence?
- What are some of the strategies people use to try to mask their lack of confidence?
- What's the earliest age a child could become aware of confidence?

Conflict

- Are you comfortable with some level of conflict, or do you prefer to avoid it completely?
- Have you had any conflict situations at work?

- Over what kinds of issues did you fall out with your parents when you were a teenager?
- Imagine you had bought a small electrical appliance that didn't work when you got it home. When you took it back you weren't given a refund as the store staff said it looked like you had dropped it. You haven't dropped it. What would you do?

(G) Disagreeing (1)

It's not uncommon to disagree with people's views, and there are several ways to deal with this depending on the level of disagreement, and how you want to tackle it.

One way is to do nothing. You may decide it is not a major issue and that it's more useful to let the conversation flow. That's okay.

- Is there much conflict between you and your partner?
- Does marriage counseling work?
- What would you do if you had a husband who got annoyed with you if you didn't have the evening meal ready for him when he got home, even though you both worked full time.
- If a child thinks one of their parents hasn't behaved well (and is justified in this) should the parent go into "time out" or have some similar consequence?

(G) Disagreeing (2)

If you disagree with what someone has said and decide to say something, the responses can range from humorous, light-hearted, and polite to rude and aggressive.

The type of response you choose will usually determine the type of reaction you'll get.

- When small children bicker, what's the best way to deal with it?
- Can we learn any helpful strategies from how politicians handle conflict in debates?

Coping strategies

- Do you have a coping strategy for times when something unexpected happens and you know you will be late for an appointment?
- Do you have a coping strategy for when you go to a funeral?
- Do you have a coping strategy for times when you have to say goodbye to people you like and will miss, when *you* are leaving or moving away?
- Do you have a coping strategy for times when you have to say goodbye to people you like and will miss, when *they* are leaving or moving away?
- Do you have a coping strategy for times when you lock yourself out of the car or house?

(G) Giving support

You can give support to someone by staying with the topic the other person is talking about, rather than moving onto something different. Letting them talk further on the issue shows your concern. For example: *"It's really hard when things like that happen. What are you thinking of doing now?"* or *"It was frustrating wasn't it?"*

- Do you have a coping strategy for times when you are ill and need to spend time in bed and there are people or pets to look after or commitments you can't fulfill?
- Do you have a coping strategy for times when someone makes disparaging remarks about you that aren't true?
- Do you have a coping strategy for times when you lose something such as your cell phone or purse?
- Do you have a coping strategy for times when you suffer from lack of sleep?
- Do you have a coping strategy for times when someone around you is very angry?

Creativity
- Would you describe yourself as a creative person?
- In which creative field are you most talented? Music, art, writing, dance, food, crafts, etc.
- Give an example of your most creative problem solving!
- What kinds of creative people do you have a respect for?

(G) Starting a conversation—fast or slow?

Some people like to take time at the beginning of a conversation to get to know people and connect with them, while others are happy to get started without the "social niceties." The slower starters may see others as a bit brusque, while the faster starters may want to hurry the others along. Neither is right or wrong, it's simply a matter of personal style, and one that's useful to be aware of.

- Think of someone you would like to organize a surprise celebration for. Devise a fantastic event.
- Your friends are getting married. He is an architect who likes music, and she is a history teacher who likes animals. You have been asked to design a suitable, fun, wedding cake. What would you design?
- You've been offered a free place on a weekend creative course of your choice. What would you choose?

(A) Succinct, full or rambling answers (1)

How you answer a question depends on a number of factors—the type of question, the type of answer the person expects, the situation, your personality and so on. Sometimes a succinct answer is all that's needed.

If the question is a closed question, you may only need to simply answer *"Yes"* or *"No"* or give a short reply, and then let the other person speak again.

- You have to raise enough money to buy kitchen equipment for a local charity. Think of an innovative way to do this.
- Choose a room in your house. If you had to decorate it in a completely different, but recognizable,

style, what style would you choose and how would it look?

- Imagine you are writing a children's fiction book. Create a new type of character.

Dating

- Dating—love it or loathe it?
- What was your worst date ever?
- Who were the people you shouldn't have dated?

(Q) Open vs. closed questions (3)

Open questions often start with "Who," "What," "How," "Why," "When," "Tell me about," "Describe," or "What do you think of." They tend to lead to longer answers.

Example

Topic: Dating

Starter: Compare *"What do you think of online dating?"* which requires a longer answer, with *"Would you try online dating?"* which could be answered with a *"Yes"* or *"No"* response.

- It was your first date, you had a good time, but they didn't call you back. Have you had this experience, and if so what did you do?
- How do you, or did you, choose clothes to wear on a date?
- Did you treat any of your dates badly?

(Q) Impolite questions (1)

Most people want approval, and it's possible to ask a question in a way that works against this and is in fact a put down.

For example if a person answered the question *"How do you, or did you, choose clothes to wear on a date?"* with *"Actually I'm going on a date at the weekend and I've just bought a new red dress."* If you respond with *"You're not going to wear red are you?"* this is likely to be seen as a put-down.

- What was it like falling in love?
- What do you think of online dating?
- Have you ever been stood up?
- What are the best and worst pick-up lines you've heard?

Do you like . . .?

- Do you like having midnight snacks?
- Do you like looking in the mirror?
- Do you like relaxing in the bath with a glass of wine?
- Do you like going to the gym?
- Do you like classical music?

(Q) Open vs. closed questions (4)

Sometimes it's good to ask a closed question first so you can clarify, and then go on to ask a more open question to get the other person thinking. A rough guide is to use one to three closed questions per open question.

Example

Topic: Do You Like . . .?

Starter: *Do you like going to the gym?*

This is a closed question and may produce a *"Yes"* or *"No"* response, which means you can then ask another closed question or two and/or an open question based on their answer.

For example, if *"Yes"* you may ask *"Which one?" "How often do you go?" "What have been the main benefits?"*

If *"No"* you may ask *"Don't fancy it then?" "What kinds of activities do you do to keep fit?"*

- Do you like keeping a diary?
- Do you like entertaining people at your home?
- Do you like eavesdropping?
- Do you like being out in the sun?
- Do you like yourself?

(A) Succinct, full or rambling answers (2)

Don't give succinct answers all the time as it makes it hard work for the other person and the conversation will become very stilted. If you have a tendency to do this, try to fill out some of your answers, even when people ask you closed questions. An expanded answer gives the other person a hook they can latch onto so they can carry on the conversation.

For example if they ask *"Do you like being out in the sun?"* instead of simply saying *"No"*, pad it out a bit. *"Not really. I usually avoid being out in the sun as I'm very fair skinned and I burn easily."* This will give them a hook (skin types) so they can bring this topic into the conversation.

Dreams and hopes

- Describe your dream job or career.
- What were or are your parents' hopes for you?

- What would be your vacation of a lifetime?
- Who has been the person who has most believed in you, and what did they want for you?

(Q) Succinct, full or rambling answers (3)

Sometimes full answers are the best way to go. These are answers that are not too short nor too long or rambling, but give a satisfactory, on-topic answer.

Example

Topic: Dreams and Hopes

Starter: *What were or are your parents' hopes for you?*
A succinct answer could be, for example, *"They wanted me to become a doctor,"* while a full answer would make more of a story of it—what they wanted, why they wanted this, what you wanted, how you resolved it . . .

- What dreams and hopes do you have for someone close to you?
- Describe someone you know who is living their dream.
- How would you finish this off: I hope that by next year . . .
- Are your partner's hopes and dreams compatible with yours?
- Dream big! What would you really love to do, be or have but haven't dared to dream that big?
- My hope for the next generation is . . .

Education

- What do you think of the education system today?
- What has been the most useless subject you've ever studied?

- What are the main skills you have learned in the "school of life" that you didn't learn at school?
- Looking back, what were the best things about your school?

(Q) Subjective and objective questions (1)

A subjective question asks for your opinion, an objective question asks for specific information. There's generally no right or wrong answer to a subjective question, simply what your opinion is.

Example

Topic: Education

Starter: *What do you think of the education system today?* If it were an objective version of this question, it may ask you to describe the current education system.

- If you could be paid to study anything you wanted, what would you study?
- In which subjects did you get your best grades at school?
- Who was the best teacher you've ever had?
- I don't think there's a single teenager leaving college these days who can read and write properly. Don't you think so?

(Q) Winding people up

Only do this if you can say it tongue in cheek, knowing that the people there will see the funny side of it, otherwise you may start an argument!

For example, if you were with a group of teachers:

Topic: Education

Starter: *I don't think there's a single teenager leaving college these days who can read and write properly. Don't you think so?*

- How would you finish this off: If I were Secretary of Education I would ...
- How do you think we could improve the education system to make students more prepared for the world of work?

(Q) Subjective and objective questions (2)

An objective question asks for specific information, whereas a subjective question asks for your opinion. It's expected that the information you give is correct.

Example

Topic: Education

Starter: *In which subjects did you get your best grades at school?* If it were a subjective version of this question, it would ask what you thought you were best at.

Either / Or

Which of these choices appeals to you more? Explain your thought process and what you think the choice will give you:

- Either a weekend in a chalet in the mountains or a weekend with a good book on the beach.
- Either a free subscription to a healthy lifestyle magazine or a free subscription to an alternative lifestyle magazine.

- Either an hour with a current political leader of your choice or an hour with an historical figure of your choice.
- Either a free membership for the gym or a free course of dance lessons.
- Either a night out at the opera or a night out at the filming of your favorite TV program.

(G) Giving support—sympathy

You can give emotional support by showing sympathy for others, for example, *"Oh you poor dear, that must have been terrible for you."*

Sympathy is different to empathy. Empathy is when you can understand what the other person is feeling because you have has a similar experience or can put yourself in their shoes. Sympathy is acknowledging the other person's emotional challenges and providing comfort.

- Either a tour of a prison or a chance to share lunch with children in an orphanage.
- Either a working vacation in a vineyard overseas or a working vacation at a refugee camp.
- Either a chance to foster a child for a weekend or the opportunity to donate $10,000 to a worthy cause of your choice.
- Either a chance to influence the country's prison system or a chance to influence the country's spending on the military.
- Either a chance to go back in time and amend something you wish you hadn't said or a chance to go back in time and find something you have lost.

Emotions

- What never fails to make you laugh?
- What never fails to make you irritated or angry?
- Do you generally have a tendency to keep your emotions under wraps, or do you wear your heart on your sleeve?
- When choosing a movie, would you prefer one that's emotionally charged or a humorous one?

(A) Succinct, full or rambling answers (4)

Do you tend to give very long answers, speak much more than others, and regularly go off on tangents? What do you think others may think of this?

Full answers are okay, though rambling ones are harder for people to keep interested in.

- Describe a situation that makes you feel very nervous.
- If you were going to be part of a very large crowd, say at a concert or sports event, how would you feel?
- When you think of the main festival of your year, for example Thanksgiving or Christmas, what emotions does this bring up for you?

(G) Avoid excluding others (1)

If you are in a group, be aware of not spending too much time talking about a topic one of the people can't contribute to. It may be that all the people work for the same organization except one, and you are talking about work issues; or that a person has recently moved into the area and you are talking about something familiar to people in the neighborhood; or that you are talking about something that happened a while ago and they are too young to know about it.

While the topic is being discussed, it's polite to explain to the person the background to it.

- Tell us about an emotional time you had at an airport or train station.
- What makes you feel really, really happy and contented?
- Talk about something or someone that is very, very cute.

Entertainment

- Tell us about the most recent live show or concert you went to.
- What are your favorite kinds of TV or radio programs?
- Would you generally prefer to go to the cinema or to the theater?
- Does the cost of a night out put you off going out?
- What's the most unusual or interesting entertainment event you've been to?

(G) Being considerate

Mentally check from time to time that the words, tone of voice, expressions and body language you use are not likely to cause offense.

Offense can be caused in a number of ways, sometimes without realizing it. For example dismissing an interest that someone has *"You don't watch that TV program do you?"*, or the beliefs they have, or the culture they belong to.

Offense can arise from such actions as pointing at people in an accusing way, looking bored, turning away or raising an eyebrow.

- Do you use the internet as a form of entertainment?
- What do you think of events such as the Oscars?
- Do you have a favorite celebrity?
- Why are so many people fascinated by every aspect of a celebrity's life?
- Is there a certain kind of person who goes to the opera or the ballet?

(Q) Are you fishing for the answer you want?

Fishing for an answer is where you have an opinion and are looking for confirmation of it, rather than asking a question to seek the other person's views.

Example

Topic: Entertainment

Starter:*What do you think of events such as the Oscars?*

NOT: *What do you think of those appalling events like the Oscars? Isn't it just a group of overpaid celebrities strutting around in expensive designer gear?*

Family and Family Life

- Tell us about growing up with your parents.
- How is your relationship with your parents now, or while they were still here?
- When I was a child I wish my parents had . . .
- How do you get on with your siblings?
- Tell us about your grandparents.

(Q) Avoid being judgmental

Keeping a question open, with ideally a positive or at least a neutral slant on it, will allow for more rapport and a more positive answer.

Example

Topic: Family and Family Life

Starter: *How do you get on with your siblings?*

NOT: *You've got three sisters; I'm guessing you must have a lot of sibling rivalry?*

- Is there a distant relative you'd like to have more contact with?
- What do you wish you'd said to a family member before they died?
- Which member of your close or extended family is most like you?
- Who is the most unusual member of your family?
- Tell us about your favorite family photos.

Family Finances

- What are your main priorities regarding the family finances?
- Has your financial situation had an impact on your decision to have children?
- What advice would you give to a young couple with a baby regarding managing the family finances?
- Do you argue with your partner about how money is spent?
- Between you and your partner which one of you is most prone to impulse buying?

(G) Enthusiasm (1)

People are drawn to enthusiastic people, so the more enthusiastic you can be while you're talking the more people will be drawn into the conversation. Even a topic that others aren't initially interested in can become fascinating if you speak with passion and enthusiasm. Enthusiasm is contagious!

- Between you and your partner which one of you is more bothered about social image?
- If you and your partner had to agree on which expenses to cut, which areas would you decide on?
- Are you saving for anything at the moment?
- Money is a very emotional issue. Do you know what your partner's feelings about money are?
- If you had a child with dyslexia and had enough money to either send them on a special course or have a family vacation, which would you choose?

Fashion, Clothes, and Makeup

- How would you describe your clothing style?
- What kind of clothes would you never wear?
- Does being fashionable have to cost a lot of money?
- Shoes!
- How much of the clothing you possess do you actually wear?

(Q) Play devil's advocate to get a lively conversation going

Playing devil's advocate is when you take a stance you don't necessarily agree with for the sake of debate, humorous or otherwise.

Example

Topic: Fashion, Clothes, and Makeup

Starter: *Does being fashionable have to cost a lot of money?*
You could answer with a reply such as *"Of course it does! No one can be fashionable without wearing the latest designer clothes. There is no other way".*

- How many places do you have to store your clothes, and what have you got in there?
- When it comes to makeup, do you tend towards the minimal look or do you go the whole nine yards?
- Do you shop at thrift shops?
- Do you keep up with fashion trends?
- People will think you're a bimbo if you have high fashion clothes and wear lots of makeup. Agree?

(Q) Starting with a contentious topic (1)

It's okay to use a contentious starter if you want to begin a lively conversation. If you want to create an impact, you can be as contentious as you like! However, always remember to be sensitive to people's needs.

Example

Topic: Fashion, Clothes, and Makeup

Starter: *People will think you're a bimbo if you have high fashion clothes and wear lots of makeup. Agree?*

If you know there are people in the group who have very different views on this, or if there are people in the group with very different clothes and makeup styles, this could be a contentious starter.

(Note that in other instances, it may be a simple, fun starter designed to produce some light-hearted humor. Not everyone will have the same reaction to a topic; some people may not see it as contentious at all. The meaning of something depends on the context.)

Fears

- What's your biggest fear?
- What fears did you have when you were younger?
- Do you have a niggling doubt that's always there?
- Do you have any phobias?
- Are you afraid of getting old / older?

(G) Listening skills: I-listening vs. You-listening

Be a "You-listener" rather than an "I-listener."

I-listeners are people whose aim is to turn everything round so they can talk about themselves, while You-listeners are more interested in hearing what the other person has to say. People like to be listened to, and you will be seen as a much better conversation partner if you are a You-listener.

Example

Topic: Fears

Starter: *Do you have any phobias?*

Person A: *Since I was a child, I've always been terrified of bees and wasps.*

Person B (I-listener): *Me too, I hate the way they always seem to fly round my head, especially when I'm out at a picnic. There was one time when . . .*

Person C (You-listener): *Poor you. Do you know how this started?*

- Are you afraid of dying?
- What is something that most people are afraid of, but you aren't?
- Which of these would you be most afraid of and why:
  o Having a spider crawl on your face
  o Getting lost in a foreign country where you can't speak the language
  o Walking across a swing bridge one hundred meters high over a river
  o Spending a night in a haunted house?
- What's a good way to banish a fear?

(Q) Problem solving questions

A problem solving question asks for action, ideas, and suggestions.

Example

Topic: Fears

Starter: *What's a good way to banish a fear?*

Flirting

- Do you flirt, or have you ever flirted?
- Do you notice if someone flirts with you?
- Do you like it when someone flirts with you?
- Does your husband or partner flirt?
- If someone attractive started flirting with you today, what would you do?

(G) Avoid excluding others (2)

If in a group, be aware of spending time having an open conversation with one other person, when it should be a topic for a conversation for just the two of you. For example discussing plans with another person, when the topic isn't relevant to anyone else.

- How did you start your current or most recent relationship?
- Do you get jealous if someone flirts with your partner?
- Who's the most flirtatious person you know?
- What's a subtle way to flirt?
- Is harmless flirting okay?

Food and Drink

- If someone were to describe you as a great cook, what would you say?
- Are TV cooking programs of any use? I don't think anyone would make the food those TV chefs make!
- Are cola drinks safe to drink?
- Did you learn any useful cooking skills at school?
- Do you like wine?

(Q) Saying something you don't believe

If you say something you don't believe, and know that others are likely to agree, it's a good way to energize the conversation when done in a humorous way. Say it with a smile and a twinkle in your eye!

Example

Topic: Food and Drink

Starter: *Are TV cooking programs of any use? I don't think anyone would make the food those TV chefs make!*

- What are your top five favorite drinks?
- If you had invited friends or family for a special meal, what would you make?
- What kind of food could you not eat, no matter what?
- Fast food or slow food—which is better?
- The Western world wastes so much food, yet there are people who are starving. Should we do anything about it?

(G) Criticism and encouragement

People who are skilled at criticism will also be capable of putting others down and making them feel demotivated and unhappy. It's hard to maintain a good quality of relationship when criticism is present.

If you identify with this, consider the alternative: encouragement. Even a few words of encouragement can build people's energy and motivation, and will lead to much happier and strengthened relationships.

Friendships

- Who is your longest standing friend?
- Do you make friends easily?
- Tell us about someone who was a friend but who is now an ex-friend. What happened?
- Who do you know who has an unlikely friendship, and why do they seem mismatched?
- What are your husband's or partner's friends like?

(G) Open vs. closed questions (5)

Open questions give the other person a chance to give more than one word answers. Being able to use open questions to keep the conversation going is a good conversational skill to have. Specifically practice using them in conversation, for example *"Tell me about . . ." "How did that happen?" "And what did your boss say about that?" "And then you . . .?"*

- What makes for a good friendship?
- Are there boundaries to a friendship?
- Do you think that your husband or partner should also be your best friend?
- Can an animal be equally suitable as a friend?
- What's the difference between a friend and an acquaintance, and what needs to happen for an acquaintance to become a friend?

(Q) Good communicators ask questions

Good communicators are interested in other people and their lives. They are not nosy, they are genuinely interested in others, and so they ask questions to find out about the person and build a greater understanding of them.

They create a base of knowledge about the person so that they have a wider range of topics to talk about, and consequently build a greater rapport.

To build these skills, try asking one additional question each time you are in conversation with someone. Just one.

Fun

- If you could live for a week as someone completely different to you, such as an explorer in the wilds of Indonesia, a housewife with ten children, or a pop star, what kind of person would you like to be?
- If you were in an improvised play and had to chat someone up, what's the most ridiculous line you could come up with?
- What's the most fun you've had with your clothes on?
- Tell us about an event that was supposed to be serious but ended up being lots of fun.

(G) Tell stories (1)

People love to listen to stories, especially funny or self-deprecating ones. Making people laugh with a story about the time you got something majorly wrong, for example, is a guaranteed winner.

It's good to introduce stories in the natural flow of the conversation by saying something like *"Speaking of unusual experiences..."* or *"I know what you mean; something like that also happened to me last week..."*

Don't rush your story, and especially remember to have a dramatic pause at appropriate moments.

- What's your idea of a fun night out?
- What's your idea of a fun night in?
- If you were asked to organize a Family Fun Day at the local community center, what would you include?
- Tell us your funniest incident.

(G) Punch lines

Do you jump in to deliver other people's punch lines? Stop!

No one likes to have their thunder stolen, and it doesn't do *you* any favors either.

- You are holding a party and want to invite someone who will liven things up. Who would you invite and what do you expect they would they do?
- What's the funniest practical joke you've been involved in?
- Tell us some material from your favorite comedian.
- Think of something you attend that isn't usually fun, but could be, such as a staff meeting, committee meeting or family get-together. How can you bring some fun into it?

(Q) Feel free to make amendments

If you can't or don't want to answer the question in the way it has been asked, it's okay to make changes and answer on a slightly different tack.

Example

Topic: Fun

Starter: *Tell us some material from your favorite comedian.*
"Actually the funniest person I know is my brother, and there was a time when he had us rolling on the floor laughing when he . . ."

Health

- Which do you prefer, alternative or traditional medicine?
- What is your parents' and grandparents' health history like?
- What's been the worst health issue you've had to cope with?
- Are you a hypochondriac?
- If you had a significant health issue and a new drug had been created to treat it, would you be a guinea pig in the drug trials?

(G) What else is going on for people?

Issues that are happening in people's lives may have an impact on what people say or how they say it, and may not be typical of how they would normally converse.

For example if the other person speaks very negatively of the education system, it may be because their child is having difficulties at school. If they give an antagonistic answer to the question *"Are you a hypochondriac?"* they may have recently had a health scare. If they sound overly enthusiastic and extremely talkative regarding the question about their best vacation ever, they may have just come back from the holiday of a lifetime.

We don't always know the background information so we may have to give some leeway, or simply ask.

- If you had to give one piece of advice on staying healthy, what advice would you give?
- Have you had to nurse anyone through ill health?
- Has disability played a part in your, or your family's, life?
- What Old Wives' Tale do you believe in?
- Does being happy keep people healthier?

Hobbies and Interests

- Is there something you've been interested in all your life?
- What's the most unexpected interest you have?
- If you were stranded on a desert island, which of your hobbies would you miss the most?
- Have you got time in your life for another hobby?

(G) Interrupting (1)

There are different types of interruption, some positive and some not so positive.

If you want to add, in a positive way, to what's being said, it's okay to interrupt someone while they are talking, the polite way being to acknowledge your interruption. For example *"Sorry, can I interrupt for a moment? I've just heard that there will be three extra people coming."*

When you have finished speaking, invite them to continue what they were saying *"Thanks, please carry on."*

- Which person most closely shares one of your hobbies?
- Do you collect anything?
- Is there a hobby you'd like to do, but don't or can't?
- Are your hobbies expensive?
- Could you, or do you, make money by doing your hobby?

House and Home

- Tell us about the house(s) you were brought up in.
- If you could have an additional home somewhere else, where would you choose?
- Whose house do you most admire?

(G) It's okay to talk about yourself

Some people don't like to talk about themselves because they feel it's not polite. They aren't interesting enough, or because they're reluctant to share details about themselves. Their tendency is then to inundate the other person with questions, or say very little.

However it's okay to open up and share something of yourself, as that is how real connections are made. You don't need to share very personal details, but enough that the other person feels they are connecting with you. Remember that most people are interested in other people.

- If you could have one major addition to your house, free of charge, what would you have?
- How did you choose the place you are now living in?
- Which is your favorite room in your house?
- Describe your housekeeping style.

(G) It's not okay to talk about yourself all the time!

If you are the kind of person who likes to have the limelight all the time and talk about yourself, remember that balance is important in a conversation, and that other people have things to say too. A conversation is a dialogue, not a monologue.

- What are your favorite pieces of furniture and how did you acquire them?
- Do you look forward to going home after you've been away?
- What makes a house a home?

In my Wildest Dreams!

*Let your imagination run wild! What would happen in your wildest dreams if there were no boundaries and no repercussions? What would you **really** do?*

- In my wildest dreams this is how I would spend my perfect twenty-four hours ...
- In my wildest dreams, where I had as much money as I wanted, I would ...
- In my wildest dreams this is what I would look like ...

(G) Two ears, one mouth

Epictetus, Greek sage and philosopher, said in the first century AD. *"We have two ears and one mouth so that we can listen twice as much as we speak."*

It's not uncommon for people to feel that they are not adequately listened to, that they are interrupted, that their views are ignored, or that people are not listening to the *essence* of what they are saying.

Epictetus's words are equally as valid today as they were two thousand years ago. Being a good listener is a highly beneficial conversational skill.

- In my wildest dreams this is how my love life would be ...
- In my wildest dreams this is the seduction scenario ...
- In my wildest dreams this is what my house would be like ...
- In my wildest dreams my day-to-day life would involve ...

(G) Smile!

People like smiley people. Some people are fortunate and are naturally smiley, while others may need to make a little effort. Smiling must be genuine; people can tell a non-genuine smile.

Smiling can show the other person that you are interested in what they are saying. Smiling helps encourage the conversation. Smiling will make people warm to you.

- In my wildest dreams these are the people I would spend time with . . .
- In my wildest dreams I would be able to . . .
- In my wildest dreams I would be . . .

International Issues

- Given that the United States has a huge influence on the rest of the world, is there an argument for people other than Americans having a say in the election of the president?
- How has the issue of the world's response to Syria's chemical warfare shown the relative importance and influence of the United States, Russia, Great Britain, France, and the United Nations?
- Nelson Mandela endured twenty-seven years of imprisonment, subsequently going on to become one of the world's most respected leaders. Was the overall effect of his being in prison a positive or negative one with regard to what he went on to achieve?
- Choose a war you are familiar with and explain what it was *really* about.
- What have been the numerous effects of sending foreign forces to Afghanistan?

(G) Balance of focus

It will make most people feel ill-at-ease if all of the conversation is focused on them or all of the conversation is focused on you. It doesn't have to be 50/50, but it does need to have some balance.

- Is international airport security too strict?
- It is a known fact, when it comes to international trade issues, that some of the goods produced for export to the United States involve the use of child laborers or forced labor. What should the US response be?
- When children attend international schools in a different country to their own, what could be the benefits for their own country when they return?
- When children attend international schools in their own country, what could be the benefits for the country?

Irritations

- What is the most annoying minor irritation *ever*?
- Is there a minor irritation that you could easily sort out but haven't gotten around to?
- Imagine you lived in an apartment and the woman in the apartment above had music playing all day long, even during the night and when she went out. How would you deal with it?

(G) Look when you listen

When people are speaking it's important that they know where the listener is looking. Some people, for example, can't carry on a conversation with someone who is reading the newspaper or looking at a screen. They think you are not giving them your full attention and feel uncomfortable about continuing to speak. Look at people to show you are listening and to show respect.

- What has been one of your success stories in dealing with an irritation?
- Which kinds of people irritate you?
- How would you finish this off: I don't let myself get irritated by ...
- The thing that irritates me most about the media is ...

(G) Interrupting (2)

It's okay to interrupt if you need clarification *"I'm sorry, can you explain that again?"* or if something significant needs to be said *"The cafe closes in ten minutes so we'll need to finish soon."*

- The thing that irritates me most about work is ...
- The thing that irritates me most about my house is ...
- The thing that irritates me most about myself is ...

Is it Appropriate ...?

- Is it appropriate for mothers to do the school run in designer clothes, high heels and makeup?
- Is it appropriate to ask your ex to your wedding?
- Is it appropriate for the man to pay for everything while a couple is dating?
- Is it appropriate to omit a previous job you didn't like from your resume?
- Is it appropriate to take a face cloth from a hotel if you need it?

(Q) Starting with a contentious topic (2)

If you want to have a harmonious conversation, especially with people you don't know well, it's best to avoid contentious issues.

Example

Topic: Is it Appropriate …?

Starter: *Is it appropriate for the man to pay for everything while a couple is dating?*

If you know that people in the group have very different views on this, it could be a contentious topic, and best avoided.

- Is it appropriate to eat meat in front of a vegetarian?
- Is it appropriate not to tip restaurant staff if the service wasn't very good?
- Is it appropriate to explain to your partner how they could kiss better?
- Is it appropriate to say grace before a meal if there are non-religious people there?
- Is it appropriate to swear in front of your teenage children?

(G) Different cultures

If someone is from a different culture, be aware that different conversation rules may apply. Some languages are influenced by their culture's views on the world, so that words and expressions may have different meanings for people from those cultures, and there may be topics of conversation that are taboo.

Some cultures, for example, see arguments as a positive and essential part of communication while others regard public disagreements as offensive.

However please be aware of stereotyping people, and remember that there are many types of people within every culture.

It's the Little Things

Sometimes we do things that are only small but make life easier; for example preparing breakfast the night before, or buying underwear a size too big so that it's comfortable, or setting a weekly reminder on your phone to put the garbage out.

- What is the first thing that comes to mind? What is something you do that makes life a bit easier?
- Do you do anything to make your morning routine easier?
- Do you do anything to make dealing with the laundry easier?
- Do you do anything to make dealing with other household chores easier?

(Q) Ask genuine questions

People don't like it when someone asks a question for the sole purpose of being able to show how superior they are. For example:

"Have you been there before?"

"No I haven't."

"Oh haven't you? We've been many times, twice in the last month, in fact."

If this is your purpose, it's best not to ask. Ultimately this way of communicating won't do you any favors as it works against building close relationships.

- Do you do anything regarding your clothing or underwear to make it more comfortable or easier to deal with?
- Do you do anything to make finding things in your bag or purse easier?
- Do you do anything to stop yourself losing things?
- Do you do anything to help you remember things?

- Do you do anything to make things easier when dealing with your children?
- Do you do anything to make things run more smoothly in the kitchen?

Leaving this World

NOTE: *Please be considerate when using this topic; it may be a sensitive area for some women. Check if it's okay to talk about these issues.*

- Are you afraid of dying?
- How big an impact has religion had on shaping your thoughts about life after death?
- Some people plan early: they work out the place(s) they would like to live, should they become restricted in their mobility or mental capability, and they also plan their funeral, so that others don't have to make the decisions for them. Have you thought this far ahead? What would you like to happen?
- If you knew, from an early age, exactly when you were going to die, how would this impact on your life?

(G) Physical touch

Some people are very "touchy" people, and like to touch others on the arm or give them a hug as a way of connecting with them. Some people are not "touchy" and don't feel comfortable if someone comes into their personal space. There are no specific rules around this, simply be aware of the differences between people and respect it. If you like personal touch but the other person doesn't, maybe lessen or stop doing it. If you don't like being touched, try not to feel offended, it's just the other person's way of showing they like you and are trying to form a bond.

- If you knew you were dying, would you have any regrets about your life?

- How do you want to be remembered?
- What is the price of life? Should people be kept alive no matter what?
- Why do some people leave this world at a very early age?
- When people have a loved one who is dying, it's said that they don't want to talk about their feelings, they simply want to express them—shock, sorrow, grief. Who could help people deal with this?
- What are your thoughts on:

  o Passive euthanasia: bringing about a person's death more quickly by changing a form of life support and letting nature take its course.
  o Indirect euthanasia: causing the death of a person, for example through administering strong pain medication, in response to a request from that person.
  o Assisted suicide: providing information or the means to commit suicide so that the person can end their own life.
  o Active euthanasia: causing the death of a person, for example by administering a lethal injection.

Let's Guess!

How well do others know you? Let them guess what you're like by asking them these questions:

- How do you think I behaved when I was a young child at school?
- What types of pictures or posters did I have on my bedroom wall I was a teenager?
- What would make me laugh till I cry?
- Am I an early riser, a night owl, or something else?

(G) Interrupting (3)

A less positive way to interrupt is to try to take over or change the direction of, and not add to, the conversation. If you do this, you are signalling to the other person that what you have to say is more important than what they have to say. It's likely to have an adverse effect on the conversation and on the other speaker, and doesn't paint you as a respectful person.

Some people are chronic interrupters, and it has become a speaking pattern for them. If this is you, don't worry, there are ways around it! The first step is to recognize you are doing it. You could ask someone to let you know when you're doing it, by giving a small cough for example. Once you're aware of it, the next step is to train yourself to wait, and let the other person finish. You may even find that they end up saying what you were going to say. It may take you a while, and you may need some strategies like biting your lip or making a note of what you want to say and adding it at the end, but it will work.

This doesn't mean to say that you should never interrupt, just that you shouldn't interrupt too much.

- If I was given enough money to buy a designer outfit, have a short vacation or get a new gadget, which would I choose?
- Do I wear sensible underwear?
- The worst kind of entertainment event someone could take me to would be ...
- Do I like cleaning, tidying and ironing?
- I chose my current or last partner because ...
- A skill I have that I don't tend to tell people about is ...

Love

- Who loved you the most when you were a child?
- Did you experience puppy love?
- Who has been the greatest love of your life?

- What has been the greatest love of your life?
- How do you know when love is the real thing?

(A) If you are uncomfortable talking about a topic (1)

If it's a topic you'd prefer not to talk about then you don't have to. You could say something like *"I'd prefer not talk about that,"* or *"I only talk about those issues with my partner,"* or *"Can we move on to another topic?"*

Do it with respect, so the other person doesn't feel offended.

- If people have more than one child, is it possible to love them equally?
- Think of a relationship you have with your partner or a family member. What could you do to bring more love into the relationship?
- When it comes to a loving relationship, are you usually quite reserved or can you love easily?
- Has anyone suffered unrequited love for you?
- Some people don't experience any love in their life. What effect do you think this would have on them?

(G) Interrupting (4)

If you find yourself regularly being interrupted, one way of dealing with it is to make a comment *"I haven't quite finished,"* or speak slightly louder and carry on, or not leave too many pauses so that people can jump in. Or, once the interrupter has finished, you can say, preferably in a light hearted way, *"As I was saying . . ."*

Marriage

- Should it be accepted practice to live together before getting married?

- What are the advantages and disadvantages of getting married vs. living together?
- Did your husband propose to you? If so, how? If not, what happened?
- Tell us about your wedding preparations.
- Tell us about your wedding day.

(G) S.T.A.Y. Stop Thinking About Yourself (1)

Often what makes us nervous in communication situations is that we worry about ourselves, how we look, what we say, and so on.

To reduce nerves, don't worry about what the other person thinks of you: Stop Thinking About Yourself! The more you focus on the other person and what they are saying, the more relaxed you will feel, and the better conversation you'll have.

This won't happen overnight; it will take some time, but is an effective way of reducing nervousness.

- When you were walking down the aisle, did you have any doubts at all?
- Did you use traditional marriage vows in your wedding?
- Did you go on honeymoon?
- Many women change their surname to their husband's. Do you like this custom?
- Many marriages end in divorce. Why?

Meeting with Friends

- How often do you meet up with friends?
- Where do you tend to meet up?
- Who usually suggests that you get together?
- What do you do when you get together?
- Do you prefer to meet with friends one-to-one or do you prefer to meet in a group?

- What kinds of activities would you and your friends
  never do?

(G) Paraphrasing

Paraphrasing is where you reword what's been said in a much shorter way.

You can paraphrase something you've said in order to summarize the main points, or you can paraphrase something the other person has said to check that you understand.

Asking for something to be paraphrased can be very useful when you don't understand—or when you have forgotten what the other person has said!

- How long have you known your longest-standing
  friend?
- Do you prefer to have all-female or mixed get
  togethers?
- If you have a male partner, does he feel uncomfortable
  about you meeting up with your girl friends?
- Tell us about the best night out you've ever had with
  friends.

Men

- Do they drive you crazy?
- What would your perfect man be like?
- Are there *real* differences between men and women?
- Some people say that men and women will never be
  equal. Agree?

(G) Develop in-jokes

For example take something funny that someone has said and refer to it again. If it works, use it again at a later date with them.

- Can heterosexual women have genuine platonic friendships with heterosexual men?
- What are the challenges of being a man in today's society?
- Why do some men get "man flu"?
- Share one of your thoughts on gay males.

(G) Use inside jokes respectfully

Please don't use inside jokes in order to exclude other people. If you do use them, explain it to the others.

- Male egos!
- It's said that gender falls on a continuum, with some men being at the masculine end of the male continuum and some at the feminine end. Think of the men in your life. Where do they fall on this continuum?

Mixed Bag

- Look at the clothes you are wearing now. If your clothes could tell a story, what story would they tell?
- Would you, or have you, proposed to someone?
- A distant relative has died, leaving you their savings of $100,000 on condition that you live in very basic accommodation for the coming year—leaving your family, job and house if necessary—doing voluntary work amongst homeless people, before you get the money. Would you do it?
- Do you swear?

(G) Swearing. To swear or not to swear?

Swearing can be a great way to build rapport ... or it can alienate you from others. It all depends on the context.

One of the main issues is to be aware of is what the group norms are: Is it generally accepted that swearing is okay? What level of reciprocity is there? How often do people swear? What degree of swearing is acceptable, from mild through to strong?

Note that swearing is more acceptable in informal rather than formal conversation.

In instances when you are repeating what someone has said where swearing is included, you don't have to repeat the words, you can say something like *"...and then he said 'You bleep bleepbleep, how dare you...'"*

- Could you kill a turkey and prepare a meal with it?
- Would you rather live in a tropical or a temperate climate?
- Is a person's character determined by nature or nurture?
- Do you think all twins have a special bond?
- What will happen if people who have been cryogenically frozen are brought back to life in fifty years' time?
- Are there too many people in the world?

(G) Incorrect paraphrasing

Misparaphrasing is when someone incorrectly rewords what you have said. For example they may say *"So, it appears that you don't agree with it at all then"* when what you said was that you hadn't made your mind up.

It may be a genuine misparaphrase, or it may be done deliberately in order to irritate you. The best way to approach this is to deal with it calmly, avoid arguing, and simply state the correct viewpoint.

Money

- If you look back over your life and were to draw a graph of the ups and downs of your finances, how would the graph look?
- Have the times when you have had the most money equated to the times when you have been the happiest?
- Do you give money to worthy causes?
- If someone could completely guarantee that you would be very wealthy if you spent the next five years working twelve hours a day, six days a week, without any vacations, would you do it?

(Q) If you are uncomfortable talking about a topic (2)

You may not trust the questioner, as you may think they are asking questions to probe, be nosy or get you to reveal information so they can gossip or respond with a put down. In these instances, you could politely refuse to answer; change the focus back to them, or move onto a different topic.

Example

Topic: Money

Starter: *If you look back over your life and were to draw a graph of the ups and downs of your finances, how would the graph look?*

If you were wary of giving a response, you could begin with a non-specific answer and then ask the same question of them: *"That's an interesting question. I wouldn't know off the top of my head and would need to think about that one. What would your graph look like?"*

Or you could begin with a non-specific answer and then amend the topic. *"That's an interesting question. I wouldn't know off the top of my head and would need to think about that one. What I have noticed though, is that the time I was earning the most was when I was in a job I was passionate about. Have you found that too?"*

- Other than the essentials of general living costs, what do you spend most money on?
- If you won a million dollars what would you do?
- Who is the biggest miser you know?
- On a scale of zero to ten for being financially savvy, where would you place yourself?
- When choosing a partner, how important is their level of income to you?
- Is it possible to have too much money?

(Q) Impolite questions (2)

Be wary of phrasing questions in a way that implies that you know better than they do as to what they should be doing.

Phrases such as "Don't you think you should" may be seen as antagonistic. For example if they answered the question "*If you won a million dollars what would you do?*" with "*I'd share it with my family members,*" and you respond with "*Don't you think you should give some of it to charity?*" this may indicate that their answer isn't as good as yours.

Movies

- Would you rather rent a movie at home or go to the cinema?
- Which movie has had the biggest emotional impact on you?
- Which is your favorite movie of all time?
- If you had a day off sick and were snuggled up on the couch, would you rather watch movies or read a book?

(Q) Add an option

You don't necessarily have to choose from the options people give you; you can choose a different option.

Example

Topic: Movies

Starter: *If you had a day off sick and were snuggled up on the couch, would you rather watch movies or read a book?*
"I don't think I'd do either of those; I'd probably spend the day doing lots of crossword puzzles."

- Is there a movie sequel that shouldn't have been made?
- Think of a good movie that doesn't have a sequel. Tell us what the sequel should be about.
- Can you watch a movie several times?

(G) S.T.A.Y. Stop Thinking About Yourself (2)

Dale Carnegie said *"You can make more friends in two months by becoming interested in other people than you can in two years by trying to get other people interested in you."*

The goal isn't to show how interesting you are, the goal is to become more interested in the other person than you are in yourself. Interesting people are people who are interested.

- Do you like to watch sad movies?
- Who are your top three movie actors or actresses?
- If you could play any part you liked in a movie of your choice, which role would you choose?

Music

- How important is music in your life?
- What kind of music do you listen to?
- What kind of music don't you like?
- When and how do you listen to music? For example, on the radio in the car, via headphones while out running ... ?

(G) S.T.A.Y. Stop Thinking About Yourself (3)

Think about the other person's needs and feelings. For example, is your conversation making them feel bored, ill-at-ease, embarrassed, offended, angry, belittled? Or might it be making them feel appreciated, recognized, happy, amused, inspired?

Don't focus solely on what you want to say, be aware of the likely effect it will have on the other person.

- Do you play a musical instrument?
- Can you sing? In tune?
- Who is your favorite singer or group?
- What kind of music did your parents listen to?
- Do you use music to create a romantic atmosphere?
- Is there a particular song that has significance for you?

Names and Numbers

- Do you have a name for your car or any other inanimate object?
- If you could change your name or add another name, what name would you choose, sensible or otherwise?
- Do you have, or did you used to have, a nickname?

(Q) Listen and learn: Asking questions

Listen to how others ask questions and take note of the techniques they use. You'll begin to notice which ones produce good responses, which produce one word answers, which make people feel at ease, smile and laugh, or feel ill-at-ease, antagonistic and so on. Make mental notes of the techniques you like and can use.

- How did you choose the names for your children?
- How did you choose the names for your pets?
- Do you constantly forget pin numbers and passwords or do you have a strategy for remembering them?
- How fast can you think in numbers? Quickly—tell me your partner's age; the number of the house you grew up in; the license plate of your first car; your previous phone number; how many days until your next birthday?

(A) Listen and learn. Answering questions

Listen to how others answer questions and take note of the techniques they use. They may for example, pause before answering; ask a question to clarify; give a detailed answer; give a vague answer on purpose; make it into a humorous situation and so on. Make mental notes of what works well and what doesn't, and build up your toolkit of answering techniques.

- What's the most ridiculous name you've ever heard?
- Do you have a lucky number?
- Is the number thirteen an unlucky number?

Other Women

- Which woman has had the biggest influence on your life?
- Which woman would you most like to be like?
- Have you been jealous of other women?
- How would you finish this off: I can't stand women who ...
- What are the women in your family like?

(G) Show you can relate to what people are talking about

People like to feel that you understand what they are talking about and can relate to what they are experiencing, or that you have had the same experience yourself. Show that you can relate to what they are talking about, though only if you can; don't fake it.

Example

Topic: Other Women

Starter: *Have you been jealous of other women?*
If they answer *"Yes"* you could say *"Me too! It's hard to cope with isn't it? What happened for you?"*

- Who do you know, or who have you met, who is the most similar to you?
- Do you have female friends who are significantly younger or older than you?
- If you were stranded on a desert island with one other woman, who would you like it to be?
- Has there been an "other woman" in any of your relationships, or have you ever been the other woman?"
- Within your society, what level of acceptance is there for gay females?

(Q) Pay people a compliment

Paying people a compliment is a great way to make people feel good about themselves and create rapport. Noticing positive aspects about a person is always beneficial.

Example

Topic: Other Women

Starter: *Do you have female friends who are significantly younger or older than you?*

If, for example, they explain that they do, you may say *"I'm not surprised; you have a great knack of getting on with everyone you meet."*

Paranormal

- Have you had a paranormal experience?
- What are UFOs?
- Do alien life forms exist?
- Do you believe that there are people who have been abducted by aliens?

(G) Disagreeing (3)

When you don't agree with what someone else is saying, always treat them with respect. It's okay to disagree with their views without slighting them. Acknowledge any areas where you are in agreement, and aim to avoid using the word "but" as it can be seen as antagonistic; use a non-negative phrase instead if possible.

Example

"I think we both agree that there are a number of flaws in their line of reasoning. How does your suggestion work in practice?"

OR *"I think we both agree that there are a number of flaws in their line of reasoning. Regarding your suggestion, we need to take into account that . . ."*

NOT *"I think we both agree that there are a number of flaws in their line of reasoning, but your suggestion is wrong."*

- What are your thoughts about Area 51?
- Is there a paranormal aspect to the pyramids?
- Can dreams predict the future?
- Can buildings be haunted by ghosts?
- Would you use a Ouija board?
- Can people be possessed?

(G) Respecting differences and fears

People have many and varied fears, and what may seem trivial to one person may be of significance to someone else.

Example

Topic: Paranormal

Starter: *Can buildings be haunted by ghosts?*

If, for example, they say they have a ghost in their house and are terrified of it, it's best to avoid saying something like *"Oh yes, we had a ghost in our last house, it was nothing, there was no point getting upset about it."*

A good rule of thumb when showing respect is to aim to see it from the other person's point of view and understand how their emotions have come about. Avoiding making judgments and asking gentle questions instead when you are not sure can lead you in the right direction.

Personality

- Which of these personality types is most like you:
    - o Impulsive, likes to talk and have fun
    - o Ambitious, likes to lead
    - o Kind, people-focused, likes harmony
    - o Thoughtful, cautious, likes perfection

- Is your husband or partner the opposite personality type to you?
- Do your main friends have a similar personality to you?

(Q) Bring in humor by saying something incorrect

Say something that's the opposite of what's true. Very amusing when people know the true answer.

Example

Topic: Personality

Starter: *Is your husband or partner the opposite personality type to you? "Absolutely! He's very noisy, never stops talking and always laughs way too loud!"* (When this is really how you are).

- Are you an introvert, an extrovert or a combination?
- Describe the different personalities of the family members you were brought up with.
- What can personality tests show?
- Is it possible to change your personality?
- What kind of people do you have a personality clash with?
- Which personality trait do you wish you had?
- Is it okay to use your personality traits as an excuse?

(Q) If you are uncomfortable talking about a topic (3)

If you feel the question requires specific information about you that you don't want to reveal, you can change the focus of your answer by making it general rather than personal.

Example

Topic: Personality

Starter: *What kind of people do you have a personality clash with?*
You could widen the focus by talking about people in general. *"You know, I was thinking about that issue recently and I've noticed that people who have the same type of personality are the ones who generally clash . . ."*

Physical Appearance

- Which part(s) of your body do you most like?
- Are you happy about how tall you are?
- Do you do anything to deal with your weight?
- Boobs!

(G) Please do not ever . . .

. . . ask a question that involves someone opening up and revealing something personal about themselves, and then treat it with disrespect later on in the conversation or at a later date. Being able to trust someone is one of the fundamentals in a relationship, and if someone exposes a vulnerability only to have it treated without respect, it can cause significant emotional hurt.

For example if the topic were *"Do you do anything to deal with your weight?"* and someone shares the struggles they've had to cope with, it would be inappropriate to bring it up later in a hurtful way *"How can you give advice on that, you couldn't even manage to control your weight?"*

- Do you like having your photo taken?
- Which do you find the most attractive skin color?
- Has your physical appearance ever been an advantage to you?

- Has your physical appearance ever been a disadvantage to you?
- Which famous person would you most like to look like?
- Be honest: do you scrutinize women's appearance and find faults?

(A) Supportive feedback

If the feedback you want to give is not positive, despite being kind, find a way to say it that provides a positive option.

For example, if you were asked *"Does this hairstyle make me look older?"* instead of simply saying *"Yes, it does make you look older"* how about saying *"If you don't feel comfortable about your hairstyle, how about we look through some magazines and see if there are any you like better?"*

Pleasure

- Can you share one of your guilty pleasures?
- What is something that you find intellectually pleasing?
- What is something that is an emotional pleasure for you?
- What is one of the most pleasurable physical sensations?
- What is your favorite sexual pleasure?
- What could or should be pleasurable but isn't?

(G) Being interested

Great conversationalists are genuinely interested in what others say, and are enthusiastic in their questioning and in their listening. When you feel that someone is genuinely interested in what you are saying, it raises the level of energy in the conversation and increases the feeling of connectedness to that person. Ask yourself if you could improve how interested you are in others and what they talk about.

- What was your greatest pleasure when you were a child?
- How can one thing cause someone so much pleasure, such as a lovely meal or beautiful music, but have no effect on someone else?
- What was something that didn't used to be a pleasure for you, but now is? What has changed?
- Some people seem to get pleasure out of hurting others. Is this "pleasure"?

Politics

- How often do you have conversations about politics?
- How would you describe your level of interest in politics?
- Would you like to be, or are you, involved in local politics?
- What should children be taught about politics in school?
- Who has been the greatest political leader?

(A) Pause before you start answering

Take a couple of seconds before you reply, especially before a weighty question. This will give you time to think through what you are going to say, and will give the impression that you are giving a considered opinion.

See the technique: *Pause—Work out your end point—Go in a straight line* from the section "How to avoid rambling" page 17.

You don't need to do it every time though, it's also okay to answer straight away when you know what you want to say.

- For the average person's daily life, does it make much difference which political party is in power?
- Which factors are important when deciding who to vote for?
- Are politicians to be trusted?
- Will a female ever be president of the US?
- Should politicians have any say in religious issues?

(Q) Use quotes

Sometimes it's useful to bring in a suitable quote to liven up your answer. It's a good idea to learn a few short ones, including humorous ones, and build them up over time.

Example

Topic: Politics

Starter: *Are politicians to be trusted?*
"I agree with Henry Kissinger who once said "Ninety percent of the politicians give the other ten percent a bad reputation.""

Possessions

- Are you a hoarder?
- If your house was on fire and you could go in and save one of your possessions, what would you save?

- What's the possession that you've lost and would dearly love to have back again?
- Tell us about a special piece of jewelry.
- Which is your most treasured photo?
- Do you have any of your parents' possessions?

(G) Do you finish other people's . . .

. . . sentences?

Don't do it! People don't like it.

You can think faster than others can speak, so sometimes you may have worked out what the other person is going to say before they've finished. However, if you finish off someone's sentence, firstly you might get it wrong, and secondly it gives the rather impolite impression that what they are saying is so obvious that you can't be bothered waiting for them to get it out!

- If you were stranded on a desert island and could have a spare set of clothes, an item of special importance, and something to keep you occupied, what would you choose?
- Would it interest you to live with very few belongings, where you had the bare minimum of (though enough) possessions?
- Do you have possessions stored away that you haven't seen for years? If so, why do you keep them?
- If a friend or family member said you were welcome to take one of their possessions and keep it as a gift, what would you take?

(G) Meaning is contextual

You obtain the meaning of what people say from the context. Some contexts are obvious. Let's say someone came in wearing a bright red hat and said "*I got it at the thrift shop for five dollars*," you wouldn't need to ask what they were referring to as the meaning is obvious.

However, some contexts are less obvious. Imagine you said to a friend, "*I'm thinking of going to a movie tomorrow, want to come?*" and they snap at you "*Of course I don't want to come.*" In this instance your context may be a simple request for a social night out. Their context may be that they've just had some bad news they are trying to cope with; or perhaps they've had an argument with someone; or they have just been asked to work late tomorrow by a boss they don't get on with.

There are many types of "invisible" contexts that can have an effect on what people are saying which may make the true meaning difficult to grasp.

In situations where someone has communicated something that doesn't feel right, before jumping to conclusions consider that there may be an invisible context you aren't aware of. You may need to gently ask.

Pregnancy

NOTE: Please be considerate when using this topic; it may be a sensitive area for some women. Check it's okay to talk about these issues.

- Was it easy for you to conceive?
- How easy was your pregnancy / pregnancies?
- Did you put on much weight when you were pregnant?
- Did you enjoy being pregnant?

(G) When not to interrupt

If someone is talking about an emotional topic or a topic that's very important to them that they need to share, the typical conversational mode of turn-taking may not apply while you let them say what they need to.

- Did you have any cravings while you were pregnant?
- Describe the birth(s).
- Were you thoroughly prepared for when the baby arrived?
- How long did it take you to lose the weight after giving birth?
- Would you like to have, or would you have liked to have, more children?
- If you are planning to have a child, are you doing anything to get your health and body ready?

Previous Relationships

- Tell us about one of your exes.
- Have you suffered from unrequited love?
- Have you been a good judge of character?
- Has infidelity featured in your previous relationships?
- How have your relationships ended?

(Q) If you are uncomfortable talking about a topic (4)

If you feel a question is inappropriate, deal with it by deflecting and giving a vague answer. Always be pleasant while you are doing so.

Example

Topic: Previous Relationships

Starter: *How have your relationships ended?*
"Oh goodness, I've been married for fifteen years now, and it's such a long time since I had another partner that I'm afraid I can't remember the specifics. I think we just grew apart."

- Do you regret ending any of your previous relationships?
- Were you deceived by any previous partners?
- Are you happy with how you behaved in your previous relationships?
- Could you go back to any of your previous partners?
- If you are divorced, do you regret marrying?

Problems

- What's the biggest problem you've had to deal with?
- What problems are you dealing with at the moment?
- Who do you call on for help?
- Who causes you the most problems?
- Do you know someone who has a problem that you would love to help them with?

(Q) Be aware of "leading" questions

Leading questions are questions where you direct the other person towards answering in a certain way, or put words into their mouth.

Example

Topic: Problems

Starter: *Who causes you the most problems?*
NOT: *Who causes you the most problems? Is it your husband?*

- Has being a woman ever been a problem for you?
- When a problem arises, what's usually your initial reaction?
- Which of your problems are you most proud of having solved?
- What kinds of problems are you skilled at helping others with?
- Some people make a mountain out of a molehill. Can you give an example of this?

Quotes about Women

Give your thoughts on these quotes:

- On the whole, I think women wear too much and are too fussy. You can't see the person for all the clutter. (Julie Andrews)
- Speaking very generally, I find that women are spiritually, emotionally, and often physically stronger than men. (Gary Oldman)
- The connections between and among women are the most feared, the most problematic, and the most potentially transforming force on the planet. (Adrienne Rich)
- A homely face and no figure have aided many women heavenward. (Minna Antrim)
- I always say God should have given women one extra decade at least, especially if you want a family. You're trying to pack a lot in. (Christine Baranski)

(Q) Don't ask a question just to be nosy

Tempting though it may be, using a starters to find out something about the other person simply for the purpose of being nosy (you will know when you are doing this!) isn't the best way to build trust and rapport.

- There are only three things women need in life: food, water, and compliments. (Chris Rock)
- As usual, there is a great woman behind every idiot. (John Lennon)
- It's not fair that women look in the mirror and feel disgust because of what society has made them believe. (Jessica Simpson)
- It's hard to tell how far women's individuality has come in the past twenty years. (Annie Lennox)
- You can find lots of people like you through technology, and women in particular like communities. (Carly Fiorina)

Quotes by Women

Give your thoughts on these quotes:

- Luck? I don't know anything about luck. I've never banked on it, and I'm afraid of people who do. Luck to me is something else: Hard work—and realizing what is opportunity and what isn't. (Lucille Ball)
- The poor give us much more than we give them. They're such strong people, living day to day with no food. And they never curse, never complain. We don't have to give them pity or sympathy. We have so much to learn from them. (Mother Theresa)

(G) Bonding: Have open body language

Keep your body language open and non-threatening and aim to look approachable. You will be perceived in a more positive light and more welcoming if you have open, rather than closed body language.

If you adopt closed body language by sitting hunched up, with arms and legs crossed and an averted gaze, it won't make you look very approachable.

- Giving birth is little more than a set of muscular contractions granting passage of a child. Then the mother is born. (Erma Bombeck)
- Self-pity in its early stages is as snug as a feather mattress. Only when it hardens does it become uncomfortable. (Maya Angelou)
- One never notices what has been done; one can only see what remains to be done. (Marie Curie)
- We do not grow absolutely, chronologically. We grow sometimes in one dimension, and not in another, unevenly. We grow partially. We are relative. We are mature in one realm, childish in another. (Anais Nin)
- I say to the young: "Do not stop thinking of life as an adventure. You have no security unless you can live bravely, excitingly, imaginatively." (Eleanor Roosevelt)
- Though the sex to which I belong is considered weak you will nevertheless find me a rock that bends to no wind. (Elizabeth I of England)

(G) The TV

If you are in a room with a TV, be careful that it doesn't cause a distraction. Consider switching the volume down, or switching it off altogether. If you are out somewhere that has a TV screen, think about moving to different seats where it won't be a distraction.

- When I buy cookies I eat just four and throw the rest away. But first I spray them with Raid so I won't dig them out of the garbage later. Be careful, though, because Raid really doesn't taste that bad. (Janette Barber)
- I have flabby thighs, but fortunately my stomach covers them. (Joan Rivers)

Reactions

How would you react if these scenarios happened to you?

- You are walking around a department store when the store detectives approach you and accuse you of shoplifting. Somehow there is a piece of jewelry in your bag or purse and the CCTV shows someone who appears to be you, taking a piece of jewelry.
- You get a phone call from a friend who has recently moved to live two hundred miles away. She is crying and says she is very unhappy and can't see the point of living until tomorrow.

(G) Mirroring

Mirroring is when your speech or body language mirrors the other person's. You can do it consciously, or it may happen subconsciously. Mirroring done well can create rapport, understanding and trust. It will also put the other person at ease.

If the person you're speaking to leans forward, you can too; if they have a fast speaking pace, you can match it; if they cross their legs, try crossing yours, and so on. It's very useful for building connections if done subtly, but don't overdo it and make it look obvious.

- You come home and find a huge bouquet of 100 roses outside your front door and an anonymous note in the mailbox telling you how precious you are.

- You were very close to your grandmother and miss her now that she is gone. She left you a picture she used to have in her living room, which you have had hanging in pride of place for many years in your living room. You have recently discovered that the picture is worth a lot of money. Finances are pretty tight at the moment and you would appreciate some extra income.

- You discover that several years before you moved into your home, a previous owner used the basement to make illegal drugs. Police think the owner buried the equipment in the garden and would like to dig up your lawn to investigate.

- You find that a number of neighbors who don't know you well start calling you by a different name, even though they know your name. When you ask them why, they say you look exactly like another woman, and ask if you have a twin sister.

(G) Put away anything that distracts

Do you get easily distracted? Are you always checking an electronic gadget, fiddling with something such as your keys, or sitting with headphones on listening to music? Put them away! If you can't see them they will be less of a distraction to you.

Letting yourself be distracted is seen as rude and gets in the way of good conversation and good connections. Give people your full attention.

- You discover that the person who performed your wedding ceremony was not qualified to do so, and so you are not officially married.
- You receive an invite in the mail from the school you went to, asking you to come and give a talk to the students as they deem you to be the most successful person they have had at the school.
- You walk into a café. There are several people sitting with parrots on their heads.
- A TV news crew comes up to you as you are walking down the street. They say they have heard that your town contains the highest number of musically-minded people in the country and ask if you would sing into the microphone.

Relationships

- Do other people interfere in your relationships?
- If your partner suggested you have separate vacations this year, how would you feel?
- Are you usually the dominant one in a relationship?
- Which is your most important platonic relationship?

(G) Sensitive information

Be aware that some people may not want their sensitive information shared with others. Saying something like *"Margaret's thinking of leaving her husband, aren't you?"* when Margaret doesn't want people to know, will cause upset and embarrassment. If in doubt, it's best to say nothing.

- Could you be 100 percent happy living the rest of your life not in a relationship?
- Is it reasonable to expect two people to stay in love forever?
- Is being in love the best reason to get married?
- What part does arguing play in a healthy relationship?
- If a couple chooses not to have children, are they missing out on anything?

(G) Turn taking

The accepted norm for conversation is that people take turns, the rationale being that conversation runs more smoothly this way. There are different ways to indicate a change of turn. These include directly asking for a contribution, for example *"What does everyone else think?"*; making a movement such as a change in sitting position; or having a falling intonation to indicate you have finished what you are saying.

A very common way to indicate your turn has finished is to look at another person to show that they can now speak.

- Can polygamy (a marriage of more than two partners) or polyamory (having more than one relationship at a time with the knowledge and agreement of all concerned) work?

Romance

- Are you romantic?
- Could you be more romantic?
- How many "true" romances have you had?
- Who has been your most romantic partner, and what romantic things did they do?

(G) Avoid excluding others (3)

You can inadvertently give the impression you want to exclude someone by sitting with your chair slightly turned away from them; with your back partly turned towards them; or by having eye contact with everyone in the group except them.

- Do you read romantic novels or watch romantic movies?
- Could you be happy in a non-romantic relationship?
- Describe a romantic surprise you gave your husband or partner.
- What's the most romantic gift you've ever received?

(G) Enthusiasm (2)

If someone looks and sounds bored while they are speaking, other people aren't going to be inspired or energized.

If the conversation covers a topic you're not particularly interested in, it's polite to try to find an aspect you can muster some enthusiasm for. Alternatively, and if appropriate, you may like to steer the conversation towards another topic.

- Is it possible to have romance without sex?
- Do women's magazines place too much emphasis on the romantic notion of a perfect life and not enough on day-to-day life?

School

- Tell us about your first day at school or your earliest memory of school.

- Which of your teachers is the most memorable and why?
- What was the funniest incident that happened at school?
- What was the worst incident that happened at school?
- What are your memories of learning to read, write or do math?

(G) Facial expression and meaning

As well as your words, your face also communicates meaning.

Ideally your words and facial expression communicate the same meaning, though not always. It's perfectly possible, for example, to say *"That's very interesting, tell me more,"* while looking thoroughly bored.

When there is a mismatch, people will believe what they see before they believe what they hear. So if your facial expression says one thing and your spoken words say another, they will believe what your face is communicating.

- Who was your best friend at school?
- Did you like school?
- When you were a young child, what happened at the end of the school day? Did someone pick you up from school and take you home?
- Do you have any school photos?
- What did you learn from being at school, over and above the academic aspect?

Secrets

- What secrets did you have as a child?
- Did you have a secret hiding place when you were young?

- Can you keep a secret?
- Have you kept a secret for someone that felt like a burden?

(Q) Don't ask a question then start answering it yourself

This may sound simple enough, though sometimes it's tempting to do it. Once you've asked a question, leave space for the other person to answer.

Example

Topic: Secrets

Starter: *Can you keep a secret?*

NOT: *Can you keep a secret? I'm sure you can. You know, I usually can, but there was a time when . . .*

- Is there a secret you've never shared with anyone that you feel it's okay to share now?
- Do you have a secret stash of chocolate (or similar) in your house?
- Have you ever kept a relationship secret from others?
- Some people are very secretive and give little away about themselves, even ordinary stuff. Why are they like this?
- What would you say is the world's best kept secret?
- What secrets does the government keep from us?

Sex

- Were you brought up to believe that sex before marriage was unacceptable?
- On a scale of zero to ten, how important is sex to you?

- Do you remember the first time you had sex?
- Would you have sex on a first date?
- Do you use sex toys?

(G) Emotions

If someone has opened up on an emotional topic, make sure they are given enough time to finish what they need to say. Please don't rush and change the topic before time. Once they are finished, it's then good to move onto a lighter topic to bring about a mood change.

- If your husband or partner suggested a threesome, how would you feel?
- Have you ever faked it?
- What's the difference between having sex and making love?
- How do you feel about prostitution?
- Is there too much sex on TV?
- Is there enough, and appropriate, sex education at school?

Shopping

- What has been your best bargain?
- How much online shopping do you do?
- What would be your perfect shopping spree?
- Do you spend too much?

(G) Helping those who ramble

Sometimes people can't help themselves losing focus and going off on lengthy tangents. Interjecting and asking good questions that keep people on track is a great way to keep a satisfactory conversation going.

> For example, if you ask *"Would you like to go to the market tomorrow?"* and the other person starts to go off on a tangent *"I would love to, but I'll have to call the electrician first because—would you believe it?—the stove blew up as I was making breakfast this morning! I only bought it last year and didn't expect . . ."* You can either let them continue with the story and ask questions about the stove, or you can wait for a suitable break and gently steer the person back on track. *"I'm planning to leave at ten o'clock. Will that give you enough time?"*

- Do you prefer shopping on your own or with someone else?
- Do you ever go out to just window shop and not buy anything?
- If you want an expensive purchase, would you save up for it, get it on credit or choose another way?
- Do you enjoy grocery shopping?
- Are you tempted by a special offer even when it's something you don't need?
- Do you like to buy the latest gadgets?

Situations

These are real situations that people have found themselves in. Is there anything wrong with them? Do we laugh them off, or should something change?

- A professional couple with a family hire a cleaner to come weekly. She turns up in a better car than the couple have.
- It's a young woman's twenty-first birthday. Her boyfriend is at medical school and offers to take her out at lunch time to celebrate. He takes her to the university to watch an operation, saying he hopes she'll find it as enthralling as he does.

(G) Understanding control

Sometimes when people are feeling insecure they try to establish control over the other person. They may do this by calling people names and making derogatory put downs such as "That's a stupid thing to do." If this happens to you, understand that it's their insecurity driving this.

It may help to remember the words of Eleanor Roosevelt: "No one can make you feel inferior without your consent."

- A daughter leaves home at age nineteen. She goes to university, gets a job, buys a house, gets married and has a child. Twenty years later a lot of her stuff is still stored at her parents' house as she says she doesn't have room for it.

- A couple in their sixties still have their forty-four year old son living at home. He has a good job but says he sees no need to move out.

- A professional man in his thirties splits from his wife. He doesn't feel he can afford to rent a place so stays in a tent in his friend's garden.

- A woman attends a training course to learn a new computer package. She is the only person who turns up. The tutor is out sick, so one of the non-teaching staff members offers to teach her what he knows about the package.

- A man working at a company calls up an electrician to do a small rewiring job. The electrician turns up with few tools and asks to borrow a drill and a hammer.

- A woman goes for a job interview at an all-male organization. They tell her they would like to offer her the job but can't as there are no female restrooms.

(G) Listening to stories

When someone tells a story—and it's usually prefaced by an indicator that it will be a story—the usual turn-taking nature of conversation stops and it's expected that you will listen to the whole story. Once it's finished normal turn-taking resumes.

- A woman goes to a local branch of her bank. It's closed. She calls them up later and is told that they have to close at lunchtime because too many customers turn up then.
- A sprightly woman in her eighties goes to the supermarket. She can't find what she needs, so asks for help. Later on she goes to see her granddaughter saying she wants to complain to the supermarket "because they treat me like an eighty year old."

Spiritual

- Are you spiritual?
- When people say they are "spiritual" and not "religious," what does this mean?
- Do you believe in angels and spirits?
- Have you been for a spiritual reading?
- What's the difference between spiritual and supernatural?

(G) Explain things simply

People will lose interest if there is a long drawn-out explanation. A short explanation in easy-to-understand language is the best way to help people grasp what you are saying. The mark of a good communicator is if people have understood their message.

- What are psychic powers?
- What happens when we die / pass over?
- Can mediums connect with people who have died / passed over?
- Can we manifest what we want?
- What are your views on spiritual healing?

Star Signs

Whether you agree with star signs or not, it can be interesting to look at the descriptions of personality traits to see if there is any correlation with who you feel you are, or the kind of person other people present as. Look at the descriptions given below and see if you identify with your star sign or can recognize the qualities in others.

- Aries, The Ram, March 21–April 19. This is a fire sign and Aries people can be fiery, opinionated, quick to anger, impulsive, driven and strong willed. They can also be creative, intuitive and passionate, as well as loyal friends and good family people with a sense of humor.
- Taurus, The Bull, April 20–May 20. Taurus people can be strong and stubborn although they can also be faithful, loving and generous. They are efficient, effective teachers, dependable and decisive.
- Gemini, The Twins, May 21–June 20. Gemini people may have a dual side to their nature and can be prone to mood swings. They like variety, have lots of interests and many talents. They like to talk and think, are inspirational, and have lots of charisma.

(G) If things get heated

In a quote from Rose Macaulay she says, "So they left the subject and played croquet, which is a very good game for people who are annoyed with one another ..."

If the conversation gets heated, have a break. Change the topic or do something different like going to the kitchen and making a cup of tea.

- Cancer, The Crab, June 21–July 22. Cancerians can be loving and family oriented, favoring a traditional home-centered life. They are good friends, faithful and kind, like to have time on their own but can be moody and over-reactive. They enjoy history.
- Leo, The Lion, July 23–August 22. Leos can be powerful and vocal. They may be inflexible, brave and head strong. However they tend to make good judgments, are good leaders, and are generous and charitable. They may keep their emotions hidden but usually operate from the principle of doing good.
- Virgo, The Virgin, August 23–September 22. Virgos can be good conversationalists, analytical and inquisitive with a sharp mind. They are socially adept and good at working in teams. However they may be opinionated, short-tempered and self-absorbed if out of balance.
- Libra, The Scales, September 23–October 22. Librans like balance, stability and justice. They are concerned about relationships and like communicating, although they may appear introverted and lacking in confidence. They can be kind, caring, and supportive.

(G) Make people feel good

It's said that people won't remember the words you say, they won't remember the things you do, but what they will remember is how you make them feel.

Making people feel good about themselves is a skill you can learn, and one that is a fundamental of excellent communication.

After an interaction, people will generally feel positive, neutral or negative about their communication with you. Aim to leave people feeling positive.

- Scorpio, The Scorpion, October 23–November 21. Although Scorpio people can be secretive, insensitive and stubborn, they can also be calm, collected and capable of great undertakings. They are determined, pay attention to detail and are not easily swayed.
- Sagittarius, The Centaur, November 22–December 21. Sagittarius people can be extroverted, generous and honest. They like life to be big. However they can be impatient, uncontrolled and intense and may undertake too many activities. They take setbacks in their stride but do not like to be tied down.
- Capricorn, The Goat, December 22–January 19. Capricorn people can be intelligent, instinctive and good at organizing. They do not like criticism but will accomplish well if they follow a plan. Faithful and sensual, they are good at helping others with their problems.
- Aquarius, The Water Bearer, January 20–February 18. Aquarians like to find new ways of doing things, and may do so in an unpredictable and flamboyant way. They can be intellectual, artistic and compassionate, taking on humanitarian causes.

(G) If you know A LOT about a topic . . .

When you are very knowledgeable about a topic and others aren't, how much do you tell people? Be considerate in how much you share, unless others are equally interested. They may not want to know every tiny detail.

You could give an overview or summarized version of your knowledge in order to gauge the level of interest, and if people are keen to know more they will ask questions.

- Pisces, The Fish, February 19–March 20. Pisceans may come across as quiet and unassuming, though they can be highly knowledgeable and generous. People may take advantage of their kind and trusting nature. They can be loving and trustworthy, a great supporter of family and friends.

Stay at Home Mom

If you are or have been a Stay at Home Mom:

- How did you make the decision to become a Stay at Home Mom?
- Did you ever regret your decision?
- What are or were the most challenging issues?
- Was it the best decision for your child / children?
- Was there any pressure for you to go back to work?

(G) Balance

Conversations generally work better when they are balanced, and people have a similar amount of speaking time. It doesn't need to be equal, but if one person dominates the speaking time, it won't be a satisfactory exchange for those who feel their views are deemed to be unimportant.

If you haven't been a Stay at Home Mom:

- What do you imagine are the benefits of being a Stay at Home Mom?
- What do you imagine are the disadvantages of being a Stay at Home Mom?
- Is it the best thing for the child?
- What would be the difference between having a Stay at Home Mom or a Stay at Home Dad?
- Is it in employer's best interests to keep the woman's job open for a period of time?

Stories

Sometimes making up a continuous imaginary story can be a fun part of conversation. Try making some of them outlandish for more effect. One person starts the story; the next person carries it on, and so on until everyone has had a go.

- I was looking online at travel deals and saw a bargain that was too good to be true . . .
- It had been a very tough day. I came home, opened the front door and . . .
- When I answered the phone my friend yelled, "You'll never believe what's happened!"
- There was a loud commotion in the shopping mall. When I went over to see what was happening . . .

(G) Intonation and meaning

You can sometimes give a different meaning by changing the word you stress, and / or the tone you use. Try saying this seven-word sentence in seven different ways by placing the stress on a different word each time you say it: *"Martha didn't say I broke the vase."*

Now try saying the sentence *"I love the works of Shakespeare"* with the emphasis on the word *"love"* in a genuine tone then in a cynical tone. Now try saying it as if there were a question mark at the end of the sentence.

You can give a range of meanings to what you say, not just by the words you choose, but by how you choose to say them.

- Deciding to treat myself, I went into the lingerie store ...
- It was Saturday night, the last night of our vacation. We were having a meal and I thoroughly expected him to propose to me ...
- Out of the blue I got a phone call from the local radio station, live on air. "You've won!" they announced ...
- In the dead of the night I heard the bedroom window being opened from the outside ...

(G) Count on your fingers

If you have a small number of points you want to talk about, hold up the corresponding number of fingers. Then touch one finger until you've talked about the first point then fold it down, then touch the next finger while you talk about the second point, and so on. It will reduce the likelihood of interruptions. Be aware of not going on for too long about any of the points. This will only work if you have a small number of points.

- I went to meet a friend at a café. When I got there I saw someone at the next table I'd been at school with many years ago ...
- I was extremely shocked when I discovered that ...

Strangers

- Have you ever been on the receiving end of a random act of kindness from a stranger?
- Have you ever carried out a random act of kindness for someone you didn't know?
- If a beggar approached you, smiled and politely asked you for just enough money to buy a simple meal, what would you do?
- Have you had any dealings with tramps?

(G) Words to help continue the conversation

If you have asked a question, the other person has given a reply and you're not sure what to say next, try using a question starting with one of the Five W's and One H: What, When, Who, Why, Where, and How.

Example

Topic: Strangers

Starter: *Have you ever been on the receiving end of a random act of kindness from a stranger?*
If they reply "Yes I have," your next question could be, for example "What happened?" "When was that?" "How did it happen?"

- Think of a female you don't know that you've seen recently, for example working at the local library, at the checkout at the supermarket, or living in the same street as you. Try describing the kind of person you think she is and how she lives. For example what are her hobbies? Where would she go on vacation? What's in her refrigerator? What magazines does she read?
- Think of a male you don't know that you've seen recently, for example working at the local library, at the checkout

at the supermarket, or living in the same street as you. Try describing the kind of person you think he is and how he lives. For example is he married? What pictures does he have on his living room wall? What are his political views? Would he have a tattoo?

- A friend of yours sponsors a child in Africa. She shares details of the child's brother, a four year old boy who is also in need of a sponsor, and asks if you could help. Would you sponsor him?

(G) Explaining who people are

If you talk about people that others don't know, it's respectful to explain who they are. Saying *"Celeste is coming with me tonight"* and carrying on the conversation when people don't know her relationship to you, is not as helpful as saying *"Celeste, my colleague from work, is coming with me tonight."*

- Have you ever stopped to help a stranger?
- You get on a long-journey bus, train or coach and there are two empty seats. One is next to a nun in her thirties and the other is next to a teenage boy holding a bird in a small cage. Who would you sit next to and why?
- You are out with a friend when she bumps into one of her male friends, and you all go for coffee. Her friend is a part time art lecturer at the university and a part time artist. He says he finds your facial features interesting and invites you to his studio so he can paint you. Would you go?

Stress

- Is stress a modern day phenomenon?
- Do you use any strategies to avoid stress?
- What's the most effective way you've found to deal with stress once it's happened?
- When things go wrong, do you have a tendency towards anger or towards depression?
- Do you tend to panic?
- Imagine that you have been invited to write a magazine article or record a podcast on "How to keep calm when everything around you is falling apart." What would you say?

(G) Laugh!

Laughter, surprisingly, isn't so much about humor; it's more about relationships. Fundamentally, people like to laugh because it makes them feel they belong, are accepted, and have a good bond with others.

This, fortunately, means you don't *have* to be good at telling jokes or even telling humorous stories (though those are very useful skills), because ordinary comments are capable of producing laughter if said in a happy, light-hearted or mischievous way. People love to laugh; it's contagious, it's universal, and it has many benefits. It makes you feel better, it helps you remember things, it stimulates and makes you more alert, it helps you relax, and people will warm to you if you make them laugh.

It's important to have genuine laughter—people can tell when it's not—and to laugh *with* others, not laugh *at* others. Laughing *with* shows inclusion, laughing *at* indicates exclusion.

It's also okay to laugh at something you've said yourself; that's very common, and people appreciate it.

- What is the main thing that causes you to feel stressed?
- Who is the main person that causes you to feel stressed?
- Laughter is said to be a good antidote to stress. How much laughter is in your life?
- Which of the following would cause you to feel the most stress and why:
  - Getting caught in traffic and being late for a job interview
  - Having your purse stolen
  - Being wrongly accused of shoplifting
  - Being trapped in an elevator

Support

- If you need emotional support, who or what would be your first port of call?
- If you were having financial difficulties, what would be your preferred form of support?
- One of your female friends is starting out on a new business venture and asks for any support you can give. What is the main type of support you could offer?
- Do you use books or other forms of written material when you need help over a personal issue?

(G) Bonding: Use eye contact to create a connection with others

It's very hard to create a connection with someone else if you don't look at them. All you need to do is hold the other person's gaze for a few seconds at a time, every now and then. Don't hold their gaze for too short a time that you come across as shy and uneasy in conversation, or for too long a time that they feel you are staring at them.

- Which member of your family generally needs the most support?
- Do you provide support to people other than your family or friends?
- What could be the benefits of having a mentor?
- If you were asked to be a mentor, what type of life issues do you feel most qualified to help others with?
- Who is a person you wouldn't go to for support?
- If you are part of a group of female friends, what happens when one of the group is going through a challenge and needs support?

Technology

- What kind of cell phone do you have and why did you choose it?
- Are items such as cars, ovens, washing machines and microwaves becoming too complex to easily operate or repair?
- I couldn't live without my . . .
- Do you have a favorite technology brand?
- Some women feel that technology companies "dumb down" their marketing to women and make it a bit "pink." Agree?

(G) Matching emotions

People like to feel that there is some sharing of emotions, particularly when the topic is an emotional one for them. If you look distanced from their feelings it will make it hard for them to open up or relate to you.

In order to create rapport, make your facial expressions, body language and way of speaking tie in with their emotions. If they are excited look happy, perhaps lean forward; if they are upset look sympathetic and make comforting sounds such as "oh dear," or maybe touch their arm; and so on.

- It's said that when it comes to games consoles, women from mid-twenties to mid-thirties play more games than men. What's the attraction?
- The dangers of technology for teenage girls.
- Should technology stores have more female assistants? Or at least male assistants who understand how to deal with women?
- What has been the greatest technology advancement in recent years?
- What has been the least useful technology advancement in recent years?

Teenage Years

- What happened when you hit puberty?
- Tell us about the highs and lows of your life as a teenager.
- Learning to deal with periods—how was it for you?
- Skin problems!
- Did you get into any trouble during your teenage years?

(G) Exaggeration

Obvious exaggeration is a great way to bring in humor.

Example

Topic: Teenage years

Starter: *Skin problems!*

"Wow, did I have skin problems. The geography teacher would use my face as a map of the Rockies!"

Use exaggeration sparingly though; if you overdo it, it will wear thin after a while.

- Did your parents like the friends you had?
- Who were your heartthrobs?
- Did alcohol and drugs feature in your teenage years?
- If you could go back in time to when you were a teenager, what advice would you give yourself?
- What's the difference between teenagers these days and teenagers in your day?

Temptation

- What's the temptation you can't resist?
- Is food a temptation for you?
- Is alcohol a temptation for you?
- Is there a person you can't resist?
- Have you ever been tempted to run away and start a new life?

(Q) Say something outrageous or humorous

If it's not a serious topic and you want to make the conversation livelier, say something ridiculous, and not necessarily true!

Example

Topic: Temptation

Starter: *What's the temptation you can't resist?*
"I love going round my local supermarket and secretly putting expensive items into people's shopping cart when they're not looking. Anyone else like doing this?"

- What is the one thing you would never be tempted to do, no matter what?
- Have you gained strength from things you've managed to resist?

- Think of something that's a temptation for you. What could you do to plan ahead in order to reduce the risk of giving in?
- Looking back, which temptation do you really, really wish you hadn't given in to?
- George Orwell said that "Many people genuinely do not want to be a saint." Agree?

The Common Good

The common good is a concept that looks at setting society up in such a way that the conditions are to everyone's advantage, rather than supporting individuals or groups selfishly fighting to meet their own needs. Although not everyone will agree on what constitutes the common good, it's generally agreed that with some simple sacrifices, positive steps are possible.

- What can be done to make forward movements towards an affordable, good quality health care system?
- What can be done to make forward movements towards reducing the carbon footprint?
- What can be done to make forward movements towards having clean air and an unpolluted environment?
- What can be done to make forward movements towards litter-free environments?

(G) Focus on what people are saying!

If you are an I-listener (page 68) it's going to be useful to learn to listen to what others are saying *without* focusing on what *you* want to say. Try some You-listening!

Yes, there will be occasions when there is something you are bursting to say and so don't listen to everything that the other person is saying. That's fine. What's needed is a greater proportion of You-listening than I-listening.

- What can be done to make forward movements towards a more effective education system?
- What can be done to make forward movements towards better public safety?
- What can be done to make forward movements towards reducing poverty?
- What can be done to make forward movements towards a fair and unbiased legal system?
- What can be done to make forward movements towards the issue of working women and suitable child care?
- What can be done to make forward movements towards caring for elderly people?

The Future

- Are you looking forward to the future or are you concerned about what the future may bring?
- If you were able to find out what would happen in your future, would you?
- Are you an optimist or a pessimist?
- Malcolm X said "Tomorrow belongs to the people who prepare for it." Have you been sowing any seeds to harvest in the future?
- When is the future . . . when does it start?

(Q) Vulnerability

Displaying a level of vulnerability and talking about something that may be perceived as a weakness can indicate that you trust the other person to respect this aspect of you. It can be a very powerful technique for building a strong level of rapport between people, if used well.

However, be careful to use this technique wisely. Don't use it too much and avoid using it too early on.

Example

Topic: The Future

Starter: *Are you looking forward to the future or are you concerned about what the future may bring?*

"To be honest, I'm quite worried about the immediate future as I've just taken on a big mortgage and now I'm not sure that my job is safe. What on earth will I do if I lose my income?"

- Have we been visited by people or beings from the future?
- When it comes to people, would you say that the best predictor of their future behavior is their past behavior?
- How would you finish this: A year from now . . .
- For society as a whole, is the future looking more promising than the past?
- Give your prediction for what the world will be like 100 years from now.

Time

- What is your biggest time stealer?
- Are you an early, on-time, or late person?
- Do you procrastinate? And if so, when?
- A quote from Doug Larson states, "For disappearing acts, it's hard to beat what happens to the eight hours supposedly left after eight of sleep and eight of work." Agree?

(G) Body language

The signals sent by a person's body language do not have a fixed meaning. The meaning for each signal will depend on the context. For example someone who is yawning may not be bored, they may be genuinely tired or on medication that causes drowsiness. Someone who has their arms crossed may be very cold rather than closed or defensive. Different cultures may give different meanings to body language aspects.

When trying to understand what someone's body language means, it's best not to rely on just one clue, but to use several clues to get a sense of the real meaning.

- Do you find it easy to give of your time to other people?
- In your life at the moment, is time passing slowly or quickly?
- What time of the day do you function best?
- Do you ever get so absorbed in something that you don't notice time passing?
- Is there going to be enough time left in life to accomplish everything you want?
- Is time a great healer?

Treating Yourself

- Do you spend time and money on giving yourself a treat?
- What do you do when you want to totally relax?
- You've been given some money as a birthday present in order to treat yourself. How would you spend it?
- A friend has offered to treat you to a meal at a restaurant of your choice. Where would you go and what would you like to order?

(G) Be careful with "why" questions

If you ask too many, or ask them in an insensitive way, "why" questions can sound confrontational or hostile. "why" questions have the potential to put people on the defensive. There are times when they are not the friendliest way to ask a question, and there may be a kinder alternative.

Example

Topic: Treating Yourself

Starter: *Do you spend time and money on treating yourself?*

If the person says *"No, I don't tend to treat myself,"* and you respond with *"Why don't you?"* it may sound rather harsh, even if it is a genuine question.

A kinder way could be *"And would you like to?"* or *"Oh dear, what can we do about that?"*

- It's your birthday and you've taken the day off work. How are you going to spend it?
- Would you view spending money on furthering your education as a "treat?"
- Do you put yourself last after your husband or partner, the children, and maybe even the family pet?
- Are you good to yourself? Do you treat yourself as well as you would treat a friend?
- If you've made a mistake do you berate yourself or treat yourself with compassion? Could you treat yourself more lovingly?
- Do you worry that if you give yourself a break and accept your imperfections that you might become self-indulgent?

(Q) Obvious questions

Sometimes questions seem so obvious that you wonder why people ask them. For example if someone is sneezing, blowing their nose and looks full of a cold, they ask *"Are you okay?"* or if someone has a very obvious new outfit they ask *"New outfit?"*

If someone asks you an obvious question, note that these are not questions as such even though they are phrased that way. They are simply a means of connecting with you, introducing a topic of conversation and giving you a way to start talking about it.

Truth and Lies

- What has been the most hurtful lie someone has ever told you, and how did you deal with it?
- Has there been a time when telling the truth got you into trouble?
- If you were with a couple, both of whom were friends of yours, and the wife told a lie about where she was the previous evening—she was with another man— would you say anything?
- Is there an issue you've buried your head in the sand about because you don't want to know the truth?

(G) Etiquette

The fundamentals of etiquette, no matter the culture, are to respect others' point of view and treat people the way you would like to be treated. This means that if you wouldn't like to be on the receiving end, then don't do it yourself. Aim to behave in a way that is comfortable to others, while understanding that most people are simply seeking friendship, kindness, and peaceful relationships.

- Would you believe a newspaper with a tagline "Truth every day"?
- When is telling a lie the best thing to do?
- Sometimes something is a lie, sometimes something is the truth, and sometimes it's neither of these. Give an example of this.
- When is it a good idea to use a lie detector?
- At what age do children become capable of telling a lie? Why would they start to tell lies?
- Given that a lot of history wasn't well documented, how true can we assume most history books are?

Understanding Behaviour

People behave in certain ways, possibly because of their beliefs, or past experiences, or in an attempt to meet their needs. Read about these people and say what may be underpinning their way of behaving:

- A couple who get married and want to have a large family, at least twelve children if not more.
- A woman who fills in her diary with many, many activities. If there is a blank space she fills it with another activity.
- A man who has reached a high level in a company and who enjoys the work. A new CEO starts whose ideas and philosophy the man doesn't agree with, so he leaves his job without another to go to.

(G) Using your phone

Do you use your phone when you are with others? It's seen as impolite to spend a lot of time on your phone while you are having a conversation. It gives the impression that the person on the end of the phone is more important than the people you are with.

If there is a genuine reason and it's important to check, for example, that the children are all right, that's seen as different to having a casual phone conversation with a friend when you are with someone else.

- A couple with two children, where the wife wants another child and the husband doesn't. They can't come to an agreement.
- A jealous husband who thinks his wife is up to no good during her lunch break. He hires a private investigator to follow her every lunch time for a fortnight. The investigator finds that the wife simply goes shopping, to the library or to a café for lunch.
- A single woman who moves into a new house, who is happy and content with her life situation. The neighbor, whom she doesn't know, comes round to warn her to "keep away from my husband."

(G) Personal space

There are socially agreed norms in societies as to the amount of personal space that is acceptable when conversing with others. For example the space for family and friends is around 18 inches to 4 feet (45cm to 120cm); while the space for intimacy is much closer, and the social distance space is around 4 to 8 feet (1.2 m to 2.4 m). If you sit or stand too close or too far away, it will make people feel uneasy.

- A grandfather who is babysitting his young grandson. The grandson loves to watch the same DVD over and over, but the grandfather gets annoyed and says he can watch it only once.
- The parents of a twenty year old female who check on her every movement, even though she gives them no cause for concern. They check her cell phone, her email and even how many miles she has traveled when she borrows the car.

(G) Accuracy

It's not a good idea to bluff and pretend you know something if you don't. If you're not completely sure of the accuracy of your information, you can add a rider such as *"As far as I know..."* or *"The last I heard was..."*

- A couple who decide to emigrate, leaving all their family. One of their relatives tells them it is a selfish, stupid thing to do and that they should do what all the other family members have done and stay in the place where they were born.
- A husband who pretends to be happily married. However he is having a relationship with another woman for whom he has bought a house and a car, and spends as much time with her as he can.

Vacations and Travel

- Do vacations play a big part in your life?
- On the continuum from budget vacations through to luxury vacations, which type do you prefer?

- Before you go on vacation, how much planning do you do?
- How much of your country or the world have you seen?

(Q) Choosing questions in a conversation lull

If the conversation dips pick a topic that you know the other person is interested in, even if it's something you don't know anything about. If you show genuine interest, the conversation will liven up. It could be their hobby, family, new job, project they're working on or an association they belong to.

Alternatively, if you don't know them well, choose a generic topic such as *"What are your plans for the weekend?"*

- What has been your best vacation ever?
- Where's the most exotic place you've been to?
- If you could spend a year traveling the world, where would you go?
- Would you rather have a city, beach, camping or adventure vacation?
- Would a vacation in temperatures of over 100 degrees Fahrenheit put you off?
- Are there issues that hinder traveling for you, such as fear of flying or travel sickness?

Weird and Wonderful

- What's the strangest thing that's ever happened to you?
- Who is your most eccentric friend?
- Did you go through a rebellious phase?

- Tell us about the most bizarre outfit you've ever worn.
- If people were to use the word "strange" to describe one of your characteristics, which one would it be?
- What is the most unusual food you've eaten?

(G) Inaccuracy

If someone says something you know isn't accurate, how you deal with it depends on the type of conversation, the level of rapport you have with them, and the importance or otherwise of the inaccuracy. Saying, laughingly *"You haven't got a clue about it, have you?"* may be the best approach for the situation; saying nothing may be suitable for another situation; whereas a more polite version such as *"That may not be accurate"* might be better for a different situation.

In general, bluntly telling people *"That's wrong"* can be seen as antagonistic.

- What is the most bizarre item you possess?
- Tell us about a strange coincidence.
- Which group of people's way of living do you find weird?
- Which group of people's way of living do you find wonderful?

What Would you Do If . . . ?

- What would you do if you opened the front door and one of your exes was standing there?
- What would you do if you found a message in a bottle on a beach, written fifty years ago by someone from another country who wrote their name and address on the note?

- What would you do if you noticed an article in your local newspaper reporting that you had won a million on the lottery, when you hadn't?
- What would you do if you were asked to take part in some research by a female university professor studying women's personal grooming habits?

(Q) Non-answers

Non-answers are replies to a question that don't give any real information. If the other person gives a non-answer, it may be because they feel uncomfortable talking about that particular topic. If you sense this is the case, move on to something else.

However some people give non-answers because they haven't heard the question properly, don't understand what you are asking, don't know very much about the topic, or are not able to express what they want to say. If you sense this is the case, try asking the question another way or move on to another topic.

- What would you do if you found an old camera hidden in the bushes in the local park; took the photos to be developed; and found they were photos of a now-famous person taken before they were famous?
- What would you do if a colleague asked you to look after her pet tarantula while she went away for a few days?
- What would you do if you got a message from a boy you had been at school with at age five, who asked if you would like to meet up?

(G) Ask for advice

People like to be asked their advice on a matter, it makes them feel valued.

If you ask someone's opinion, it may signify that you've already made your mind up no matter what they say, whereas asking for advice gives the impression you haven't yet made your mind up and value their input.

Compare *"I'm going to buy the red one. Do you think it will look okay?"* with *"Which one should I buy, the red one or the pink one?"*

- What would you do if you were asked to model clothes in a local fashion show to raise money for charity?
- What would you do if you were asked to be a model for a life drawing class?
- What would you do if you were asked to be on a radio panel interview to talk about phobias?

Wisdom

Over the years we learn about life aspects, through formal education, and especially through experience. We learn a lot from our successes and failures and by observing what other people do. What wisdom have you gained about the following issues during your life that you could pass on to others?

- Marriage and relationships. What have you learned along the way from relationships that have worked and those that haven't? What advice could you give to young people starting out?

- Friendships. What have you learned about conducting friendships so that all people gain benefit and feel positive about the friendships?

- Health. What do you now know about good health that you didn't know when you were younger? What have you done to maintain or improve your health? What would you recommend?

- Community. Through your experience, what knowledge have you gained about how people can become involved in their community or give back to society?

(G) If you don't understand ... ask

Sometimes we don't like to interrupt and so we let the other person carry on speaking ... even though we don't know what they are talking about! They may be talking about something we're not familiar with; we may have missed the start of the conversation; they may use a person's name we don't know; or they may use acronyms we're not aware of. It's probably not a good idea to nod and say *"Mm hm."* It's okay to ask.

- Spiritual. How have you gained spiritual growth throughout your life? Have you noticed different ways that people can access spirituality that work for them, even though they may not work for you?
- Money. People approach the concept of money in different ways. From your own experience and what you have observed in others, what wisdom can you pass on?
- Hobbies and leisure. What have you learned about choosing hobbies and the amount of time to devote to them?
- Work and career. Through analysing your own experiences of working life, career, and career progression, do you have advice for others?

- Education. What would be your recommendations regarding formal education and qualifications? And about life education learned from experience?
- Fun! What is your experience of what fun's all about, how much people need and how they could incorporate it into their lives?

Women Achievers

This is a list of women who have achieved in at least one area of life. What might it have taken for them to get to the level they did, and what is the impact they may have had on others?

- Oprah Winfrey, media proprietor.
- Amelia Earhart, first woman to fly solo across the Atlantic Ocean.
- Marilyn Monroe, actress.

(A) Forgetting the question

Do you ever realize, part way through your answer, that you've forgotten the question? Don't worry, this is fairly common. All you need to do is stop and ask!

- Venus and Serena Williams, tennis players.
- J. K. Rowling, author.
- Michelle Obama, first African American First Lady.
- Lady Gaga, singer, songwriter.
- Angela Merkel, German chancellor.
- Nichelle Nichols, Lieutenant Uhura in Star Trek, first black actress in a main role.
- Indira Ghandi, Prime Minister of India.

Women and Work

- Have you been drawn to female-dominated occupations?
- Have you noticed women being treated differently in the workforce?
- Have you ever felt you've been treated differently in work because you're a woman?

(G) Looking confident

You don't have to *be* confident; you just have to *look* confident.

Three simple ways to help with the look of confidence: a) Have appropriate eye contact (see "Bonding: Use eye contact to create a connection with others," page 131); b) Have open facial expressions and body language; c) Have a relaxed body manner.

If you avoid eye contact, have closed body language and fidget, you'll come across as less confident.

- If you have had children, what effect has this had on your career?
- If you were an employer, how would you feel about employing women who are likely to take time off for maternity leave?
- Have you ever used your "femininity" in a workplace situation?
- Would you be comfortable going to a male practitioner in a female-dominated occupation, for example a male midwife or a male beauty therapist?

(G) Sounding confident

You don't have to *be* confident; you just have to *sound* confident.

Three simple ways to help the sound of confidence: a) Finish many of your sentences with a falling intonation, giving the impression that you are assured in what you are saying and that your contribution has come to a close; b) Avoid fillers such as "er" and simply pause instead while you are thinking of what to say; c) Say your last sentence or the end of a sentence as if it *is* the end, otherwise it will sound like you are questioning yourself.

If you regularly end your sentences with a rising intonation so they sound like a question, use fillers such as "er" or "um" a lot, or let your sentences trail off, you'll come across as less confident.

- Are there any aspects of work that men are naturally better at than women?
- Do men or women make better bosses?
- Is there a glass ceiling for women?

Women Who . . .

You have been asked to form a 'Women Who' group. What kind of women would attend, and what would be the purpose of the group?

- Women Who . . . love to love.
- Women Who . . . feel invisible.
- Women Who . . . don't understand men.
- Women Who . . . buy too much.
- Women Who . . . love to be kids.

(G) Impromptu . . . or not

Winston Churchill is famously quoted as saying *"I'm just preparing my impromptu remarks."*

Great conversationalists will, of course, make some great impromptu remarks and tell some great impromptu stories. However, skilled communicators will also continuously work on honing their skills by doing some background preparation.

One of the ways to do this is to think through an anecdote or story you are likely to tell, and work out the best way to tell it to get the most laughs or make the most impact.

- Women Who . . . want to be feminine.
- Women Who . . . want to say no.
- Women Who . . . like midnight snacks.
- Women Who . . . can't knit, bake or sew.
- Women Who . . . have a lot to give.

Work-Life Balance

- Have you got your work-life balance as you would like it?
- What are you juggling in your life?
- Have you settled for less in some areas of your life in order to improve your work-life balance?
- What is the one thing you could do to improve your work-life balance?

(G) Building on others' ideas

When someone puts forward an idea, helping them think it through or build on it is a good way to enhance a relationship.

Example

Topic: Work-Life Balance

Starter: *What is the one thing you could do to improve your work-life balance?*
    A: *"I've thought about hiring a cleaner once a week so I can have time to go swimming at the weekend instead."*
    B: *"Sounds great, let me know when you do it and I'll come swimming with you."*

- There are 168 hours in a week. How many do you spend on work (time at work, traveling, preparing, etc.) and how many hours do you have available to do as you wish?
- Sometimes success comes at the price of balance. Are you happy to pay this price in order to have success?
- When you can't fit everything in, what is the first thing you let go?
- Do you have help with household chores and / or the children?
- When you are not in work can you completely switch off from it?
- If you work, and are in a situation where financially you could manage without working, why do you work?

(G) Give an outline before you start

If you know you've got a set number of points you want to talk about, outlining them at the beginning will help others understand, and will reduce the likelihood of interruptions.

Example

Topic: Work-life balance

Starter: *If you work, and are in a situation where financially you could manage without working, why do you work?*
"I was thinking about that recently, and came to the conclusion that there are three reasons why I work . . ."

Worrying

- Be honest, are you a worrier?
- What are the top three things you worry about?
- If you have a minor health issue, do you blow it out of proportion and imagine it to be a major debilitating disease?
- Is there something you used to worry about in the past, but no longer need to, as you've learned to deal with it or the situation has changed?

(G) Big words and acronyms

Some things get in the way of a good conversation. Using complicated words, sentence structures or acronyms may make it difficult for people to understand.

Example

Topic: Worrying

Starter: *What are the top three things you worry about?*
It's probably not a good idea to say something along the lines of "In the first instance, I find I am predisposed to worrying about feeling less than magnanimous, and for this reason I offered to assist my neighbor organize the upcoming yuletide festivities . . ." or "I always worry when I have to contact the CTO of the CFW Corp to discuss their NSP . . ."

- Do you get irritated by people who worry about trivialities?
- When you worry, does your health suffer?
- Looking back, were some of your worries in the past not worth the effort of worrying about? Were you making mountains out of molehills?
- Suggest three techniques for reducing or eliminating worrying.
- Which one of the following issues causes you the most worry: your weight; your finances; your appearance; a family member; your work; your health; your level of success; your neighbors; your relationship.

(G) Praise people

People like people who make them feel good about themselves. Finding genuine things to praise people about is a way to make them feel good and build the bonds of friendship.

For example: *"You've done really well, I'm impressed with how you've been coping with all the changes in your life this year."*

- Which of the following are you most concerned about: climate change; the state of the economy; the political situation; the education system; obesity levels; poverty; renewable energy; the health system; crime levels.

Your Call!

Fill in the blanks to make your own customized conversation starters!

- How long have you been _____?

- When was the last time you tried to _____?
- If your husband or partner asked you to _____, would you?
- Would you be surprised if _____ wanted you to go to _____ with him to her?

(G) Tell stories (2)

If it's not a serious conversation, you can tell a story and add to it by exaggerating or embellishing some of the aspects for effect, *"He took so long that I don't know how many cookies I ate while I was waiting for him, but it was in the region of three thousand ..."*

- I'm wondering whether I should _____, and I'd like your advice.
- I once read an article about people who _____. Have you ever done that?
- If you met a gorgeous _____ who wanted you to _____, what would you say?
- Have you ever _____?
- How would you describe your _____?
- I'd like to _____? Will you help?

Your Favorites & Your Starters

Here you can make a note of any of your favorite starters, and compile a list of your own questions and conversation starters.

Notes

Notes

Notes

Notes

Notes

Notes

Notes

Notes